Kotlin Blueprints

A practical guide to building industry-grade web, mobile, and desktop applications in Kotlin using frameworks such as Spring Boot and Node.js

Ashish Belagali
Hardik Trivedi
Akshay Chordiya

BIRMINGHAM - MUMBAI

Kotlin Blueprints

First published: December 2017

Production reference: 1071217

Published by Packt Publishing Ltd.
Livery Place
35 Livery Street
Birmingham
B3 2PB, UK.
ISBN 978-1-78839-080-4

www.packtpub.com

Credits

Authors
Ashish Belagali
Hardik Trivedi
Akshay Chordiya

Copy Editor
Safis Editing

Reviewer
Alexander Hanschke

Project Coordinator
Prajakta Naik

Commissioning Editor
Richa Tripathi

Proofreader
Safis Editing

Acquisition Editor
Sandeep Mishra

Indexer
Rekha Nair

Content Development Editor
Akshada Iyer

Graphics
Jason Monteiro

Technical Editor
Adhithya Haridas

Production Coordinator
Melwyn Dsa

About the Authors

Ashish Belagali is an IIT Bombay alumnus with 24 years of experience in software technology, management, consulting, and client handling. He has successfully executed offshore engagements in both onsite and offshore roles. He is known as a turnaround specialist, having turned many IT projects from red to green in a short time.

In spite of the senior positions he has handled, Ashish loves coding and has managed to stay hands-on with it. He often speaks about technology, entrepreneurship, and work effectiveness. He is a Kotlin enthusiast and has worked on several Kotlin projects. He is also the founder of the Kotlin Pune User Group.

Hardik Trivedi is a self-taught computer program writer. He has extensively worked on Android and Java since 2010 and has also immersed himself in Kotlin and JavaScript. When he is not working on client projects, he loves contributing back to the development community by spending time on stack overflow and writing tech blogs.

Hardik also mentors college students, professionals, and companies who have a keen interest in mobile app development. He is also an active community speaker. Someday in the future, you may find him owning a restaurant and serving exquisite cuisines to his customers.

Akshay Chordiya is the co-founder of BitFurther, an Android Developer by heart, and a Kotlin enthusiast. He has been working with Android for over 4 years. He is an active community speaker who is mostly found talking about Android and Kotlin.

Akshay is an avid blogger and instructor. He has a love for anything with the word "technology" in it! The vision of bringing about a change in the world through his knowledge is what makes him get out of bed every day and work on his apps and his start-up. "Doing what you love" can be said to sum up his life until now and in the exciting years to come ahead!

Acknowledgments

For me, the first thanks goes not to a person, but to a company. It is Google who inadvertently played a big role in this book. Google's announcement about Kotlin made me curious about Kotlin. I liked it more as I learned it. When I created the Pune Kotlin User Group without any publicity, many good programmers and students joined it out of their own interest. Then, at a Google Developer Group meet, I met Akshay and Hardik, who later became the co-authors of this book. Thus, again, it's Google who brought us together.

Writing this book was a journey. Finding time from our day job was not easy. There were ups and downs. But the team sailed through that because of a good camaraderie. Whenever one of us seemed to fall behind schedule, another one volunteered to chip in. There were healthy discussions on the content, which was made possible through the ability to respect and accept the other person's viewpoint.

I would like to thank my family who accommodated our erratic schedules. At times, after a long day at work, I would again open my laptop and work beyond midnight. My family understood and supported me.

I would also like to thank Captain D. P. Apte for his guidance. He has recently published a book, and his guidance was valuable in the initial stages when Packt started speaking to me about writing this book.

Finally, I would like to thank the Packt team for their guidance and patience. Working with Sandeep Mishra, Akshada Iyer, Adhithya Haridas, and Venkatesh Pai was a pleasure. We especially found that Akshada's comments were always inspiring and her appreciation kept up our spirits while writing the book. I am sure there were other people in the background who we just know as "the team". We noticed that "the team" was eager to help us and had a quick response time whenever the book needed it. It helped in issue resolution, and that made us sail through this journey with a good deal of ease.

– Ashish Belagali

About the Reviewer

Alexander Hanschke is a CTO at techdev Solutions GmbH, a technology company located in Berlin. He had worked on various Java-based projects in the financial industry over the last 8 years, before turning to Kotlin in 2016. Since then, he has applied Kotlin to all kinds of projects, including Alexa skills, blockchain clients, and Spring-based applications. He frequently speaks at technology meetups and occasionally writes articles about the various aspects of the Kotlin programming language.

www.PacktPub.com

For support files and downloads related to your book, please visit www.PacktPub.com.

Did you know that Packt offers eBook versions of every book published, with PDF and ePub files available? You can upgrade to the eBook version at www.PacktPub.com and as a print book customer, you are entitled to a discount on the eBook copy. Get in touch with us at service@packtpub.com for more details.

At www.PacktPub.com, you can also read a collection of free technical articles, sign up for a range of free newsletters and receive exclusive discounts and offers on Packt books and eBooks.

www.packtpub.com/mapt

Get the most in-demand software skills with Mapt. Mapt gives you full access to all Packt books and video courses, as well as industry-leading tools to help you plan your personal development and advance your career.

Why subscribe?

- Fully searchable across every book published by Packt
- Copy and paste, print, and bookmark content
- On demand and accessible via a web browser

Customer Feedback

Thanks for purchasing this Packt book. At Packt, quality is at the heart of our editorial process. To help us improve, please leave us an honest review on this book's Amazon page at https://www.amazon.com/dp/1788390806.

If you'd like to join our team of regular reviewers, you can e-mail us at customerreviews@packtpub.com. We award our regular reviewers with free eBooks and videos in exchange for their valuable feedback. Help us be relentless in improving our products!

Table of Contents

Preface

Kotlin is evolving rapidly as a universal language—a single language with which one can do many things and do it elegantly! It can be used to create a wide range of applications, spanning from large server applications that can take advantage of the most modern advances in parallel processing and rich internet applications (RIA) that run in the ecosystem of a web browser to Android apps and tiny applications that run within tiny IoT processors.

In May 2017, when Google announced official support to Kotlin to develop Android applications, the status of Kotlin was elevated overnight from *a nice, cool language* to *a language that needs to be taken seriously*. Shortly thereafter, the Spring framework, which is mighty on the server-side development, added Kotlin-only features. The Kotlin-favoring trend seems to have continued since then.

The vast array of applications that Kotlin can be used in and the value-add that Kotlin does in each of the cases with Kotlin-specific flavors can be quite overwhelming. This book is written to help the programmers find these in one place so as to put their hands around the diverse use case scenarios.

While there are books and plenty of online material covering the language basics, and then there are those covering single niche areas, there was nothing that could be referred to for understanding the vast spectrum of usage scenarios. This book tries to fill the void. This is a single book that can be used as a reference to these various scenarios.

This is not a theory book. It is a practical guide to creating industry-grade applications with Kotlin. Each chapter takes one moderately sized requirement in a given area and shows how to create a Kotlin application to fulfill it. It contains a complete set of instructions that a programmer can follow and learn the applications by coding them first hand. It also highlights the special uses of Kotlin features as they are applicable to the problem at hand.

Except for the first introductory chapter, all other chapters are independent of one another. You can, therefore, jump straight to the chapter corresponding to the application area that would be the most relevant for you, and dive deep into it to learn the skill quickly and put it to practice. It, thus, helps in accelerating your understanding and increasing the productivity in a short time.

We hope that the fast-growing community of Kotlin programmers will find this book immensely useful.

What this book covers

Chapter 1, *The Power of Kotlin*, is the introductory chapter. It covers why Kotlin is quickly becoming a force to reckon with. Kotlin positions itself as the smart choice to the various stakeholders, such as the programmer, the manager, and the businesses. The chapter looks at the technology and business reasons that fuel the adoption of Kotlin.

Chapter 2, *Geospatial Messenger – Spring Boot*, covers the use of Spring Boot technology to create robust server-side applications. Spring is one of the most well-known and well-respected server-side frameworks in the Java space, and Spring Boot is its less verbose and more powerful version. This chapter covers how a Geospatial Messenger application is created with Spring Boot technology using the Kotlin language.

Chapter 3, *Social Media Aggregator Android App*, is using Kotlin to create native Android apps. With Google officially recognizing Kotlin's use to develop Android apps, this is the most widespread application to use the Kotlin language. Today's mobile apps hardly work in isolation. They work with a server. This common scenario is illustrated with a social media aggregator app.

Chapter 4, *Weather App Using Kotlin for JavaScript*, explores the use of Kotlin to create rich internet apps that work within the browser. JavaScript is clearly the de facto standard language that works across all the browsers. However, Kotlin is clearly superior to JavaScript in many ways. This chapter shows how one can have the best of both worlds by doing the coding in Kotlin and, then, transpiling the code to JavaScript so that it works with the browsers seamlessly. The example that we will build is a simple weather application.

Chapter 5, *Chat Application with Server-Side JavaScript Generation*, explores how the same facility of transpiling Kotlin to Javascript can be used on the server side. JavaScript is used on the server side within the popular and fast Node.js framework. Kotlin can be used to create Node.js applications, as the JavaScript code that runs with Node.js can be generated from it. This chapter shows how to do so by creating a simple chat application.

Chapter 6, *News Feed – REST API*, covers the use of Kotlin specifically to create REST services. We will develop a News Feed application with the Ktor framework, which is a leading Kotlin-only framework used for server-side applications.

Chapter 7, *CSV Reader in Kotlin Native*, explores a bleeding edge technology—Kotlin Native—which is about compiling Kotlin code directly to platform-specific executables. Although not mature, Kotlin Native is worth watching as it quickly marches to its promise of becoming the only language to create native applications across disparate platforms such as iOS and Raspberry Pi. In this chapter, a small CSV reader utility is built with Kotlin/Native.

`Chapter 8`, *Dictionary Desktop Application - Tornado FX*, is about using Kotlin to create a cross-platform desktop application based on Java technology. Tornado FX is a Kotlin-specific framework, which is based on the most advanced Java GUI framework, that is, Java FX. This chapter illustrates the power of Tornado FX with a dictionary application.

What you need for this book

You will need to have the following:

1. JDK8 (download it from `http://www.oracle.com/technetwork/java/javase/downloads/jdk8-downloads-2133151.html`)
2. An IDE with the Kotlin plugin—you can use Eclipse (`http://www.eclipse.org`) and install the Kotlin plugin, or IntelliJ idea (`https://www.jetbrains.com/idea/download/`). The latter is more popular in the Kotlin community and is used in most of the chapters. The community edition is enough for most of the chapters, unless specified otherwise in the chapter.
3. Additional plugins may be needed to be installed into the IDE as specified in the respective chapter.

Who this book is for

This practical guide is for programmers who are already familiar with Kotlin. If you are familiar with Kotlin and want to put your knowledge to work, then this is the book for you. Kotlin programming knowledge is a must.

Conventions

In this book, you will find a number of text styles that distinguish between different kinds of information. Here are some examples of these styles and an explanation of their meaning.

Code words in the text, database table names, folder names, filenames, file extensions, pathnames, dummy URLs, user input, and Twitter handles are shown as follows: " We will break the `Result` object returned from the function and catch it inside two objects named `result` and `status`."

A block of code is set as follows:

```
var createTweet: Button? = null
createTweet.setOnClickListener({
  // Do button click operation
})
```

When we wish to draw your attention to a particular part of a code block, the relevant lines or items are set in bold:

```
fun ViewGroup?.inflate(layoutId: Int, attachToRoot: Boolean) =
  LayoutInflater.from(this?.context).inflate(layoutId, this,
  attachToRoot)
```

Any command-line input or output is written as follows:

```
npm init
```

New terms and **important words** are shown in bold. Words that you see on the screen, for example, in menus or dialog boxes, appear in the text like this: "Create a new project in IntelliJ, select **Gradle** and add the dependencies related to Spring Boot and Kotlin."

Warnings or important notes appear in a box like this.

Tips and tricks appear like this.

Reader feedback

Feedback from our readers is always welcome. Let us know what you think about this book—what you liked or disliked. Reader feedback is important for us as it helps us develop titles that you will really get the most out of.

To send us general feedback, simply email feedback@packtpub.com, and mention the book's title in the subject of your message.

If there is a topic that you have expertise in and you are interested in either writing or contributing to a book, see our author guide at www.packtpub.com/authors.

Customer support

Now that you are the proud owner of a Packt book, we have a number of things to help you to get the most from your purchase.

Downloading the example code

You can download the example code files for this book from your account at `http://www.packtpub.com`. If you purchased this book elsewhere, you can visit `http://www.packtpub.com/support` and register to have the files emailed directly to you.

You can download the code files by following these steps:

1. Log in or register to our website using your email address and password.
2. Hover the mouse pointer on the **SUPPORT** tab at the top.
3. Click on **Code Downloads & Errata**.
4. Enter the name of the book in the **Search** box.
5. Select the book for which you're looking to download the code files.
6. Choose from the drop-down menu where you purchased this book from.
7. Click on **Code Download**.

Once the file is downloaded, please make sure that you unzip or extract the folder using the latest version of:

- WinRAR / 7-Zip for Windows
- Zipeg / iZip / UnRarX for macOS
- 7-Zip / PeaZip for Linux

The code bundle for the book is also hosted on GitHub at `https://github.com/PacktPublishing/Kotlin-Blueprints`. We also have other code bundles from our rich catalog of books and videos available at `https://github.com/PacktPublishing/`. Check them out!

Downloading the color images of this book

We also provide you with a PDF file that has color images of the screenshots/diagrams used in this book. The color images will help you better understand the changes in the output. You can download this file from `https://www.packtpub.com/sites/default/files/downloads/KotlinBlueprints_ColorImages.pdf`.

Errata

Although we have taken every care to ensure the accuracy of our content, mistakes do happen. If you find a mistake in one of our books—maybe a mistake in the text or the code—we would be grateful if you could report this to us. By doing so, you can save other readers from frustration and help us improve subsequent versions of this book. If you find any errata, please report them by visiting http://www.packtpub.com/submit-errata, selecting your book, clicking on the **Errata Submission Form** link, and entering the details of your errata. Once your errata are verified, your submission will be accepted and the errata will be uploaded to our website or added to any list of existing errata under the Errata section of that title.

To view the previously submitted errata, go to https://www.packtpub.com/books/content/support and enter the name of the book in the search field. The required information will appear under the **Errata** section.

Piracy

Piracy of copyrighted material on the internet is an ongoing problem across all media. At Packt, we take the protection of our copyright and licenses very seriously. If you come across any illegal copies of our works in any form on the internet, please provide us with the location address or website name immediately so that we can pursue a remedy.

Please contact us at copyright@packtpub.com with a link to the suspected pirated material.

We appreciate your help in protecting our authors and our ability to bring you valuable content.

Questions

If you have a problem with any aspect of this book, you can contact us at questions@packtpub.com, and we will do our best to address the problem.

1
The Power of Kotlin

Our interest in the Kotlin programming language should be there because it is fast moving towards becoming the universal programming language. What is a universal programming language? From a simplistic view, the expectation could be that one language is used for all types of programming. While that may be far-fetched in today's complex world, the expectation could be adjusted to one language becoming the dominant programming language. Most certainly, it is the single, most important language to master. This book is written to help with that objective.

In this introductory chapter, we will see how Kotlin is poised to become the next universal programming language. In particular, we will look into the following topics:

- Why can Kotlin be described as a *better Java* than any other language?
- How does Kotlin address areas beyond the Java world?
- What is Kotlin's winning strategy?
- What does this all mean for a smart developer?

Historically, different languages have used strategies appropriate for those times to become the universal programming languages:

- In the 1970s, C became the universal programming language. Prior to C, the programming languages of the world were divided between low-level and high-level languages, the former being the languages that were close to machine code and the latter being ones that were more concise and worked better for human understanding. The C programming language was developed as a single language that could work as a low-level and a high-level language. The Unix operating system was showcased as one that was built ground-up entirely in C, without needing another low-level language.

- In the 1990s, Java became the universal programming language with the *Write Once Run Anywhere* strategy. Prior to Java, developers needed to create different programs to run on different platforms (different operating systems running on different hardware needed different programs to run). However, with Java, programs could be written targeting a single platform, namely the **Java Virtual Machine** (**JVM**). The JVM is available across all the popular platforms and takes care of all platform-specific nuances. The Java language became the universal language by being the language in which to write programs for the JVM.

Another two decades have passed, and the stage is all set to welcome the next universal language. Let's examine Kotlin's strategy to become that.

Kotlin – a better Java

Why is being a better Java important for a language? For over a decade, Java has consistently been the world's most widely used programming language. Therefore, a language that gets crowned as being a better Java should automatically attract the attention of the world's single largest community of programmers: the Java programmers.

The TIOBE index is widely referred to as a gauge of the popularity of programming languages. Updated to August 2017, the index graph is reproduced in the following illustration:

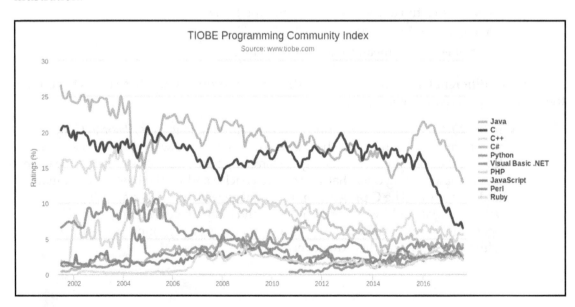

The interesting point is that while Java has been the #1 programming language in the world for the last 15 years or so, it has been in a steady state of decline for many years now. Many new languages have kept coming, and existing ones have kept improving, chipping steadily into Java's developer base; however, none of them have managed to take the #1 position from Java so far.

Today, Kotlin is poised to become the most serious challenger for the better Java crown, and subsequently, to take the first place, for reasons that we will see shortly. Presently at 41st place, Kotlin is marching ahead at a fast pace. In May 2017, Google announced Kotlin to be the officially supported language for Android development in league with Java. This has turned out to be a major boost for Kotlin, and the rate of its adoption has accelerated ever since.

Why not other languages?

Many languages prior to Kotlin have tried to become a better Java. Let's see why they could never become one.

Every language attracts the programmer community by giving them an ability to do something that was cumbersome before. Their adoption is directly driven by how much value the promise has for them and how much faith the community can put into that promise.

All languages that claimed to be a better Java and offered something worthwhile beyond what Java offers, also took something back in turn. Here are a few examples:

- .NET has been the longtime rival of Java and has supported multiple languages from day one. Based on the lessons learnt from Java, the .NET designers came up with better language constructs. However, the biggest hurdle for .NET was that it was a proprietary technology, and that created an impediment to its adoption. Also, .NET was more aggressive in adding newer language constructs. While the language evolved quickly as a result of that, it broke its backwards compatibility many times.
- Ruby (and Python) offered shortened code, enticing programming constructs, and greater expressiveness as opposed to the boring Java; however, they took away static typing support (which helps to make robust programs) and made the programs slower.

- Scala offered shortened code and advanced programming constructs, without sacrificing typing safety. However, Scala is complex and has a substantially high learning curve. It supports multiple coding styles. So, there is a danger that Scala code written by one developer may not be understood easily by another. These are risk factors for any project that includes a team of developers and when the application is expected to be supported over a long period, which is true about most applications anyway.

Why Kotlin?

Unlike other languages, Kotlin offers a lot of power over Java, while not taking anything away. Let's take a look at the following screenshot to see how:

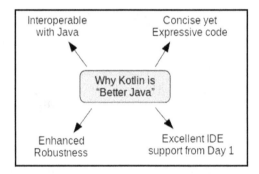

Kotlin is interoperable with Java. It is possible to write applications containing both Java and Kotlin code, calling one from the other. Calling Java code from Kotlin is simpler, as opposed to the other way around, but the former will be the case most of the times anyway, where new Kotlin code is added on top of legacy Java code. Kotlin is interoperable and can use all the Java libraries and legacy coding without having to do any code conversion. It is possible to inject Kotlin into a Java project without boiling the ocean.

Concise yet expressive code

While being interoperable, Kotlin code is far superior to Java code. Like Scala, Kotlin uses type inference to cut down on a lot of boilerplate code and makes it concise. (Type inference is a better feature than dynamic typing as it reduces the code without sacrificing the robustness of the end product). However, unlike Scala, Kotlin code is easy to read and understand, even for someone who may not know Kotlin.

Kotlin's data class construct is the most prominent example of being concise as shown in the following:

```
data class Employee (val id: Long, var name: String)
```

Compared to its Java counterpart, the preceding line has packed into it the class definition, member variables, constructor, getter-setter methods, and also the utility methods, such as `equals()` and `hashCode()`. This will easily take 15-20 lines of Java code.

The data classes construct is not an isolated example. There are many others where the syntax is concise and expressive. Consider the following as additional examples:

- Kotlin's default values to function parameters save the need to overload the functions
- Kotlin's extension functions can be used to add domain-specific functionality to existing classes, making it easy for someone from the domain to understand

Enhanced robustness

Statically typed languages have a built-in safety net because of the assurance that the compiler will catch any incorrect type cast. Both Java and Kotlin support static typing.

With Java Generics introduced in Java 1.5, they both fare better over the Java releases prior to 1.5.

However, Kotlin takes a big step further in addressing the Null pointer error. This Null pointer error causes a lot of checks in Java programs:

```
String s = someOperation();
if (s != null) {
  ...
}
```

One can see that the `null` check is not needed if `someOperation()` never returns `null`. On the other hand, it is possible for a programmer to omit the `null` check while `someOperation()` returning `null` is a valid case.

With Kotlin, the definition of `someOperation()` itself will return either `String` or `String?` and then there are implications on the subsequent code, so the developer just cannot go wrong. Refer the following table:

`fun someOperation() : String // not nullable`	`fun someOperation() : String? // nullable`
``val s = someOperation()
if (s != null) {   // null check not
needed - editor warning
...
}```	```val s = someOperation()
n = s.length() // error, null check
imposed
n = s?.length() ?: 0 // handling
null condition```

One may point out that Java developers can use the `@Nullable` and `@NotNull` annotations or the `Optional` class; however, these were added quite late, most developers are not aware of them, and they can always get away with not using them, as the code does not break. Finally, they are not as elegant as putting a question mark.

There is also a subtle point here. If a Kotlin developer is careless, he would write just the type name, which would automatically become a non-nullable declaration. If he wanted to make it nullable, he would have to key in that extra question mark deliberately. Thus, you are on the side of caution, and that is as far as keeping the code robust is concerned.

Another example of this robustness is found in the `var`/`val` declarations. Seasoned programmers know that most variables get a value assigned to them only once. In Kotlin, while declaring the variable, you choose `val` for such a variable. At the time of variable declaration, the programmer has to select between `val` and `var`, and so he puts some thought into it. On the other hand, in Java, you can get away with just declaring the type with its name, and you will rarely find any Java code that defines a variable with the `final` keyword, which is Java's way of declaring that the variable can be assigned a value only once.

Basically, with the same maturity level of programmers, you expect a relatively more robust code in Kotlin as opposed to Java, and that's a big win from the business perspective.

Excellent IDE support from day one

Kotlin comes from JetBrains, who also develop a well-known Java **integrated development environment** (**IDE**): IntelliJ IDEA. JetBrains developers made sure that Kotlin has first-class support in IDEA. Not only that, they also developed a Kotlin plugin for Eclipse, which is the #1 most widely used Java IDE.

Contrast this with the situation when Java appeared on the scene roughly two decades ago. There was no good IDE support. Programmers were asked to use simple text editors. Coding Java was hard, with no safety net provided by an IDE, until the Eclipse editor was open-sourced.

In the case of Kotlin, the editor's suggestions being available from day one means that they can learn the language faster, make fewer mistakes, and write good quality compilable code with relative ease. Clearly, Kotlin does not want to waste any time in climbing up the ladder of popularity.

Beyond being a better Java

We saw that on the JVM platform, Kotlin is neat and quite superior. However, Kotlin has set its eyes beyond the JVM. Its strategy is to win based on its superior and modern feature set.

Before we go ahead, let's list the top five appeals of Kotlin:

- Static typing (like in C or Java) means that there is built-in type safety. The compiler catches any incorrect type assignments. This makes programs robust.
- Kotlin is concise and expressive. Being concise implies that there is less to read and maintain. Being expressive implies better maintainability.
- Being a JVM language, the Kotlin programs can take advantage of the features built into the JVM, such as its cross-platform nature, memory management, high performance and sandbox security.
- Kotlin has inbuilt null-safety. Null references are famous as the billion-dollar mistake, as admitted by its inventor Tony Hoare and cost a great deal of unnecessary null-checks in programs. Kotlin eliminates those and makes the programs more robust.

Kotlin is easy to learn, especially for Java developers. Its syntax is clean and therefore easy to understand, because of which, Kotlin programs are fun for developers to code and easy to understand, and enhancing for their peers. From a business angle, they are more robust and easy to maintain for businesses.

Kotlin is in the winning camp

The features of Kotlin have a good validation when one considers that other languages, which have similar features, are also growing in popularity:

- The Crystal language attracts Ruby programmers by adding static typing support. Similarly, TypeScript adds static typing support to JavaScript and has become the preferred language for some JavaScript frameworks.
- Scala and F# add functional programming support to traditional non-functional paradigms without sacrificing type safety and, hence, are more attractive. Kotlin uses functional programming, just enough to ease out the programming in a lot of cases, but not too much to make it complex.
- Like Kotlin, Swift, and Rust also have inbuilt null-safety. Kotlin and Swift are often compared, as their syntaxes resemble one another a lot.
- Server-side languages, which were getting designed after the emergence of the parallel computing phenomena, became one of the chief requirements for providing inbuilt constructs for easing the programmer's work. One can find this in both Kotlin (coroutines) and Rust.

Go native strategy

The Kotlin developers figured that the same strategy that is used on the JVM platform could be used on other platforms too. Consider the following illustration:

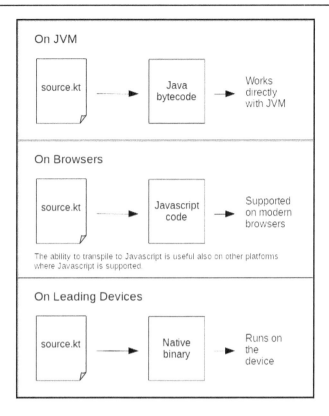

On no platform does Kotlin disrupt the platform's existing technology:

- The JVM works with the Java bytecode and Kotlin gives an alternative to Java to generate the same bytecode (By no means is Kotlin the first alternative as there are already 200+ languages that work with JVM, but it is the most elegant one for all the reasons that we have seen previously).
- On modern browsers where JavaScript is the de facto standard, Kotlin can work by transpiling to JavaScript. Again, this means that Kotlin is friendly with existing browsers without making any special effort.
- On the Node.js platform where JavaScript is used on the server side, your Kotlin code transpiles into JavaScript, and hence there are no changes needed in the Node.js framework for Kotlin to run.
- In a similar way, Kotlin/Native plans to work with other technologies in a native way. As we will see in `Chapter 7`, *CSV Reader in Kotlin Native*, Kotlin/Native will be used to generate Native code.

Since the platform's technology is not disrupted, there are zero changes needed at the platform level to adopt Kotlin. Kotlin's compatibility with a given platform can be taken for granted from day one. This eliminates a big business risk.

Kotlin's winning strategy

Kotlin's winning strategy is the sum of the various factors that we have seen previously. It has a two-pronged strategy to win over the developers with the coolness of the language, and the ease of working with it, to win over business users with its business benefits. The following illustration shows us the different benefits of using Kotlin:

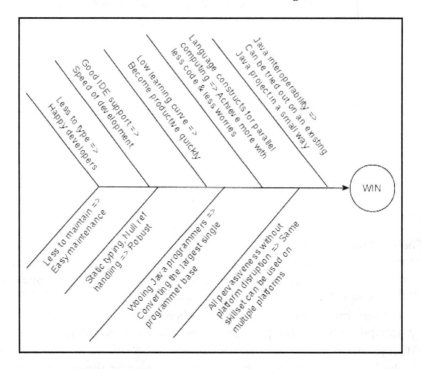

The other benefits also include:

- The growing popularity of the language
- Endorsement from Google to make Kotlin an officially supported language in May 2017
- Kotlin-specific development frameworks emerging

- Leading Java frameworks, such as Spring, offering Kotlin-specific improvements
- The growing number of applications being tried out with Kotlin
- The user groups spread across Kotlin developer hubs
- The growing number of technology companies using Kotlin

With this in mind, the winning strategy for smart programmers is to master Kotlin and learn to work with Kotlin on various platforms. Being ahead of the curve as opposed to following the world after Kotlin is already big but it will be a quick path to being recognized as a leader. Further chapters of this book will help you in exactly this mission.

Apart from going through this book, we strongly suggest you join the community.

Join the Kotlin weekly mailing list at `http://kotlinweekly.net`.

 Join the nearest Kotlin user group
at `http://kotlinlang.org/community/user-groups.html`.

Kotlin's community on Slack is at `https://kotlinlang.slack.com/`.

Summary

In this chapter, we mainly saw how Kotlin is well positioned to take off as the universal programming language. It offers an opportunity for smart programmers to establish themselves at the forefront of this rising tide.

For you to see what makes Kotlin a worthy candidate as a better Java, we saw in detail the strategies that Kotlin is employing to get there, such as wooing the largest chunk of developers (namely, the Java developers) by being a better Java and a compatible one too. In other territories, where other languages are well-established, giving code generation options to get compatible source codes/binaries. Doing everything that developers and managers love to make coding, or migrating from another language easy.

2
Geospatial Messenger – Spring Boot

Writing code in Kotlin is fun, thanks to its concise nature that allows writing applications with shorter, efficient, and expressive code. One of the biggest selling points of Kotlin is its excellent interoperability with Java which means it is designed to play well with the Java ecosystem; the frameworks and libraries.

Things get really interesting and fun when Kotlin is used together with Spring Boot, which is one of the most widely used web frameworks for quickly bootstrapping and developing web applications in Java language. Spring Boot promotes convention over configuration and thus focuses on eliminating the specification of obvious choices, making the codebase expressive and concise. As we know, Kotlin's constructs also focus on expressiveness and conciseness. Hence development with Spring Boot benefits greatly from the use of Kotlin.

It is no surprise then that with the release of Spring Boot Framework 5.0, the Spring team announced full support for Kotlin. Not only that, Kotlin specific features were also added. It is a huge step towards combining these two technologies in a simple and powerful way to quickly build web applications with a concise code base.

Through this chapter, you'll learn how to build a geospatial messenger application in Kotlin with Spring Boot technology. The best way to get the benefit of this chapter is to practice it as you go through the chapter so that you have the application running on your machine by the end.

In this chapter, we will learn:

- Spring Boot
- To build a Geospatial Messenger application with the Spring Boot Framework and Kotlin; with the database as Postgres

Why Spring Boot?

Spring is a great web framework and one of the most popular ones in the Java world. With Spring Boot it became even better. Spring Boot prefers convention over configuration and that eliminates a lot of boilerplate code. It's easier to write configurations. As a result, it feels more lightweight, unlike Spring Framework. Spring Boot is a microservice ready platform.

In a nutshell, Spring Boot helps you to quickly bootstrap your product, and it includes helpful features to push your application to production with almost no fuss.

Leveraging Kotlin in Spring Boot applications

Using Kotlin for the development of Spring Boot applications is beneficial. Let's look at some of the common Kotlin constructs that are used for building Spring Boot applications.

Extension functions

The extension functions in Kotlin provide an easy way to add new functionality to an existing API in a non-intrusive way. Often, they are used to eliminate the need to write special utility or helper classes. They make the code more idiomatic and readable.

Here is an example of where an extension function is added to the library class (java.lang.String) to check if the string is an email or not:

```
fun String.isEmail(): Boolean {
    // Logic to check if it's a email
}
```

This function will behave as a part of the String class, so you can achieve it as follows:

```
"kotlin.blueprints@packt.com".isEmail()
```

Where can the extension functions be used in the context of Spring Boot?

A case in point is where our Kotlin code needs to call the Java code and one needs to use JVM generics. But this could look ugly.

For example, here is how one would use the new WebClient from the Spring WebFlux API to retrieve a list of objects in Java:

```
Flux<Message> messages =
  client.get().retrieve().bodyToFlux(Message.class)
```

Now, for Kotlin, the code becomes (note that the type is inferred):

```
val messages =
    client.get().retrieve().bodyToFlux(Message::class.java)
```

Note that `Message::class` is a `KClass` and it needs to be converted to a Java class by adding `.java` to it. Doesn't it look ugly?

Now we could use an extension function and use Kotlin's `reified` type parameter to make the code cleaner and a workaround for JVM generics type, helping us to write or provide better APIs, as follows:

```
val messages = client.get().retrieve().bodyToFlux<Message>()
```

We now have a short and concise syntax.

> The Spring Boot Framework 5.0 ships with a few useful extension functions. Of course, you can further write your own.

Constructor injection

Dependency injection is a key feature of Spring (and Spring Boot). It reduces the coupling or in other words, makes the classes less dependent on one another. This increases the possibility to reuse them and also helps to test the app.

Spring provides three ways to inject the dependencies—Field, Constructor, and Setter injection:

- In field injection, you just declare the field and add an annotation on top of the field declaration. Although highly readable, this practice could go higher as the fields grow and also increases the dependence on a specific Spring container, thereby making testing difficult. Field injection is therefore *not* recommended.
- Constructor injection is about adding a constructor that initializes the fields and hence the injection annotations appear over the constructor. This is the preferred mechanism for injecting mandatory fields.
- Setter injection is about annotating the setter method. This is the preferred mechanism for injecting non-mandatory fields, typically to override default settings.

Between field injection and constructor injection, most Java developers use field injection (with all its associated problems). This is because constructor injection in Java has a lot of boilerplate code that makes it look bloated:

```
@RestController
@RequestMapping("/message")
public class MessageController {
  private MessageRepository repository;
  public MessageController(MessageRepository repository) {
    this.repository = repository;
  }
}
```

In Kotlin, constructor injection looks clean, light, and concise; and the boilerplate is all gone. Here is the Kotlin equivalent of the preceding code:

```
@RestController
@RequestMapping("/message")
class MessageController(val repository: MessageRepository) {
}
```

So, now there is more reason for developers to say goodbye to the field injection.

 Since Spring Framework 4.3 there is no need to use the @Autowire annotation in the case of a single constructor class.

Leveraging Null safety

NullPointerException is the most dreaded exception a developer can face when working with Java language. Sometimes it's quite difficult to trace and resolve it. Kotlin comes with a built-in Null safety system that is aimed at eliminating the null references from code:

*The null references are famously known as The Billion Dollar Mistake (*https://en.wikipedia.org/wiki/Tony_Hoare#Apologies_and_retractions*) as their inventor later called it.*

This Null safety system by Kotlin makes the whole Spring Framework API null safe (at least from the Kotlin side) and allows us to deal with null values at compile time rather than throwing `NullPointerException` at the runtime:

> *Kotlin's Null safety also means that the web apps you build with Spring Boot will be more robust.*

Functional bean declaration DSL

In Spring, we register our beans either using XML or the `@Configuration` and `@Bean` annotations. When Spring Boot is used from Kotlin, there is a new alternative to declare the beans using lambdas, which act as `FactoryBean`.

Registering beans in Java:

```
GenericApplicationContext context = new
  GenericApplicationContext();
context.registerBean(Message.class);
```

With DSL style and reified type parameters, the Kotlin equivalent is as simple and beautiful as the following:

```
beans {
  bean<Message>()
}
```

Now that we understand the key constructs of Kotlin while building Spring Boot applications, let's move on to the example application.

Let's build our geospatial messenger

We are going to build a geospatial messenger to understand how to build a Spring Boot application with Kotlin and how to leverage language features of Kotlin to enable faster development. We will learn how to build robust apps while having fun with the concise syntax of Kotlin.

The idea of the geospatial messenger is to provide a layer of maps to the end user where they can leave messages on a particular coordinate, which can be read by anyone accessing the website.

Preview

The preview of the UI of the application is shown, where the current location of the user is shown with the marker (depends if the user allows accessing location in the browser) and the envelope icon in the image denotes the messages left on a given coordinate:

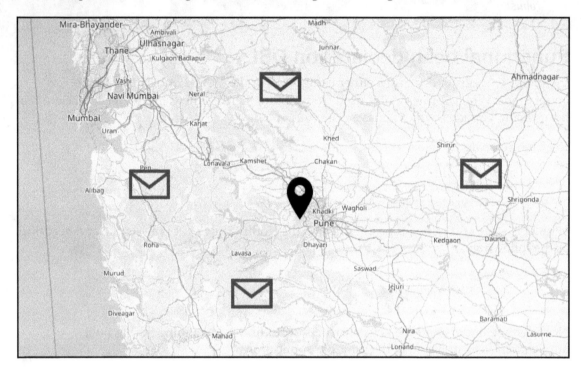

Features

Let's look at all the features we need to develop in our application:

- To leave a message, the user needs to click on a location or co-ordinate of their choice, type their message in the message box and save
- To see an existing message, the user needs to click on the envelope icon and the saved message is shown:

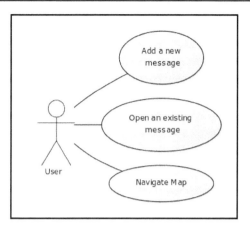

Architecture

Here is the technology stack we are going to use:

- Frontend:
  - Basic **HTML**
  - **CSS** with Bootstrap framework
  - **JavaScript** with a **jQuery** plugin
  - **Open Layers**: To show the map to the user
- Backend:
  - **Spring Boot**
  - **Kotlin**
- Database:
  - **PostGIS**: Extension of PostgreSQL for geospatial operations
  - **Exposed**: ORM for SQL operations

The following illustration is a representation of the technology stack we will use:

Setting up the IDE

We will be using IntelliJ Ultimate throughout this chapter to build the geospatial messenger application. You can use any other IDE like Eclipse or download IntelliJ Ultimate from the following link: `https://www.jetbrains.com/idea/download/`.

Creating a project

Create a new project in IntelliJ, select **Gradle** and add the dependencies related to Spring Boot and Kotlin mentioned in the following screenshot.

Here are the following steps:

1. Open IntelliJ.
2. Click **File** | **New** | **Project**.
3. Select **Gradle** with Kotlin and web:

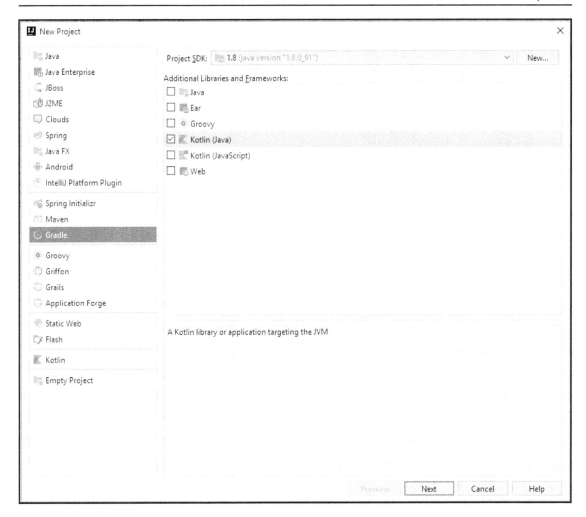

You can also use: `https://start.spring.io` to create a starter template with Spring Boot, Kotlin, and Gradle as our build system.

Project structure

The project contains two modules:

- `main` module: This contains the development code
- `test` module: This contains tests for the application

The main module contains:

- Kotlin directory (similar to Java) where all the Kotlin is placed (note that it is not enforced that the Kotlin code goes into the Kotlin directory, but it is a good convention to follow. In case you place it under another directory, then make sure to make appropriate changes to `build.gradle`).
- Resources directory contains static resources such as HTML, CSS, JS, and images for the web application.

Here is the package structure with the base package as `com.book` that we follow. Feel free to follow a similar structure in your projects:

- `db`: This contains database related code (Exposed library code)
- `domain`: This contains our data classes or model classes
- `repository`: This contains our repository classes which abstract the database interaction
- `utils`: This contains Extensions functions and some utility functions
- `web`: This contains the URL controllers

The following screenshot shows the project structure:

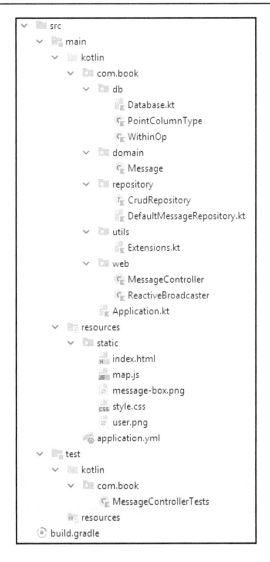

For this project, we are going to use Kotlin v1.1.50, which is the latest version at the time of writing and IntelliJ IDEA to build the application.

Setting up the build script

Build systems are software tools designed to automate the process of program compilation such as Maven, Gradle, and others. We will be using the Gradle build system for our project.

Adding Kotlin dependency

Kotlin language is added as a Gradle dependency in the project:

```
// Kotlin
compile "org.jetbrains.kotlin:kotlin-stdlib-jre8:$kotlin_version"
```

Adding Spring Boot dependencies

To set up the project with Spring Boot packages we need to add the following dependencies in the `build.gradle` file:

```
// Spring
compile 'org.springframework.boot:spring-boot-starter-web'
compile 'org.springframework.boot:spring-boot-starter-jdbc'
compile 'org.springframework.boot:spring-boot-devtools'

testCompile "org.springframework.boot:spring-boot-starter-test"
```

Exposed library

> *It is a prototype for a lightweight SQL library written over JDBC driver for the Kotlin language. It does have two layers of database access: typesafe SQL wrapping DSL and lightweight data access objects.*
>
> *- JetBrains*

It provides a type-safe SQL DSL API that allows you to define your SQL tables and describe your SQL requests with a fluent API without requiring code generation.

It supports the following dialects:

- PostgreSQL
- MySQL

- Oracle
- SQLite
- H2

Gradle dependency

We need to add an additional Maven repository in our `build.gradle` file to fetch the artifacts from the Exposed library:

```
repositories {
  ...
  // For Exposed library
  maven { url "https://dl.bintray.com/kotlin/exposed" }
}
```

Add the following dependencies for the Exposed API and another dependency to configure transaction support in the application:

```
// Exposed
 compile 'org.jetbrains.exposed:exposed:0.8.5'
// For transaction support
 compile 'org.jetbrains.exposed:spring-transaction:0.8.5'
```

Defining the table

To define a table you need to create an object with the required fields and extend the `Table` class and Exposed will create the table in the database for you with the fields as columns:

```
object Messages: Table() {
  val id = integer("id").autoIncrement().primaryKey()
  val name = varchar("name", 100)
}
```

It will result in the following query called by Exposed:

```
CREATE TABLE IF NOT EXISTS Messages (id INT AUTO_INCREMENT NOT
 NULL, name VARCHAR(100) NOT NULL, CONSTRAINT pk_Messages PRIMARY
 KEY (id))
```

Currently Exposed doesn't have support for data classes and the repository pattern. It requires the creation of an object of the required structure.

Connecting to the database

We can connect to the database with Exposed by passing the URL of the database and its driver:

```
// Connect to the database
Database.connect("jdbc:h2:mem:test", driver = "org.h2.Driver")
```

CRUD operations

The following code snippet shows an example of how to do **create**, **read**, **update**, **delete** (**CRUD**) operations with Exposed:

```
transaction {

  // Insert new message
  Messages.insert {
    it[name] = "Hello Kotlin Developers!"
  }

  // Update an existing message
  Messages.update({Users.id eq 1}) {
    it[name] = "Hello Spring-Kotlin Developers"
  }

  // Delete the messages table
  drop(Messages)
}
```

It results in the following queries:

```
INSERT INTO Messages (name) VALUES ('Hello Kotlin Developers!')
UPDATE Messages SET name='Hello Spring-Kotlin Developers' WHERE
 Messages.id = 1
DROP TABLE Messages
```

Get all the users from the database:

```
for (message in Messages.selectAll()) {
  println("$message[Messages.name]}")
}
```

It will result in the following query:

```
SELECT Messages.name FROM Messages;
```

Now it must be pretty clear how to use the Exposed library for Spring and how it works internally.

 The reason for using the *Exposed* library instead of Spring JPA is because, at the time of writing, there is no official support for Kotlin data classes and JPA, that is Spring Data JPA. JetBrains noticed this and they released their own SQL ORM library called Exposed.
Read more at `https://github.com/JetBrains/Exposed`.

Explaining PostGIS

PostGIS is a spatial database extender for PostgreSQL (`https://www.postgresql.org`) object-relational database. It adds support for geographic objects allowing location queries to be run in SQL.

It adds several geographical features on top of PostgreSQL such as extra types for geometry, geography, raster, and a few others. For this application, the geospatial support that it provides is relevant. However, readers are advised to explore this extension in depth in case they are going to be dealing with the PostgreSQL database.

Installation

We need to install PostgreSQL on our system to use it. The following are the steps on how to install PostgreSQL:

1. First, install PostgreSQL from `https://www.postgresql.org/download/`.
2. Then install PostGIS from `https://postgis.net/install/`.

 Remember the password specified while installing PostgreSQL and the database name specified while installing PostGIS because we need those details later to connect to the database from our Spring application.

Gradle dependency

We need an extra dependency for PostGIS in `build.gradle` to get the data-structures and support for connecting to the PostGIS database:

```
compile "net.postgis:postgis-jdbc:2.2.0"
```

Object mapping

In order for frontend and backend to communicate, we use some form of common language (mostly JSON). In our case, we will be using JSON for communication between backend when some action is performed from the frontend (using JavaScript-jQuery). We convert the JSON to objects, which are understood by our backend, using an object mapping library. In this, we will be using the popular Jackson library for object mapping.

We are going to add an additional dependency for object mapping of the PostGIS data-structures.

Gradle dependency

Adding dependency for Jackson-Kotlin:

```
// Object Mapping
compile "com.fasterxml.jackson.module:jackson-module-kotlin"
```

For PostGIS:

```
compile "com.github.mayconbordin:postgis-geojson:1.0"
```

The artifact of this library is on JitPack. Hence we need to add an additional Maven repository in our `build.gradle` file:

```
repositories {
    ....
    // To fetch object mapper for PostGIS
    maven { url 'https://jitpack.io' }
}
```

Completing the Gradle script

Similarly, we add more dependencies of the pre-requisite components. You can look at them in the complete Gradle script `build.gradle`:

```
group 'com.book'
version '1.0-SNAPSHOT'

buildscript {
    ext.kotlin_version = '1.1.50'
    ext.spring_boot_version = '1.5.7.RELEASE'

    repositories {
```

```
    mavenCentral()
  }
  dependencies {
    // Kotlin-Gradle Plugin
    classpath
      "org.jetbrains.kotlin:kotlin-gradle-plugin:$kotlin_version"
    // Opens all the classes - Explained later
    classpath "org.jetbrains.kotlin:kotlin-allopen:$kotlin_version"
    classpath
      "org.springframework.boot:
      spring-boot-gradle-plugin:$spring_boot_version"
  }
}

apply plugin: 'kotlin'
apply plugin: "kotlin-spring"
apply plugin: 'org.springframework.boot'

sourceCompatibility = 1.8

repositories {
  mavenCentral()
  maven { url 'https://jitpack.io' }
  // For Exposed library
  maven { url "https://dl.bintray.com/kotlin/exposed" }
}

dependencies {
  // Kotlin
  compile "org.jetbrains.kotlin:kotlin-stdlib-jre8:$kotlin_version"

  // Spring
  compile 'org.springframework.boot:spring-boot-starter-web'
  compile 'org.springframework.boot:spring-boot-starter-jdbc'
  compile 'org.springframework.boot:spring-boot-devtools'

  // Exposed
  compile 'org.jetbrains.exposed:exposed:0.8.5'
  // For transaction support
  compile 'org.jetbrains.exposed:spring-transaction:0.8.5'

  // Object Mapping
  compile "com.fasterxml.jackson.module:jackson-module-kotlin"
  compile "com.github.mayconbordin:postgis-geojson:1.1"

  // Database
  compile "org.postgresql:postgresql:9.4.1208"
  compile "net.postgis:postgis-jdbc:2.2.1"
```

```
   // Testing
   testCompile group: 'junit', name: 'junit', version: '4.12'
   testCompile "org.springframework.boot:spring-boot-starter-test"
}

compileKotlin {
  kotlinOptions.jvmTarget = "1.8"
}
compileTestKotlin {
  kotlinOptions.jvmTarget = "1.8"
}
```

 Recently the Gradle Team announced support for writing the Gradle script in Kotlin instead of Groovy lang. Read more about it at `https://blog.gradle.org/kotlin-meets-gradle`.

Coding the application

Our project is ready with required project structure and Gradle dependency and configuration. It's time to write the application code.

Frontend

The UI or frontend is made with pure HTML, CSS, and JS with jQuery.

HTML

We just have a single HTML page called `index.html`:

```
<!DOCTYPE html>
<html>
  <head>
    <title>Geospatial Messenger</title>
      <!-- CSS -->
      <link rel="stylesheet"
       href="http://openlayers.org/en/v4.3.3/css/ol.css"
       type="text/css">
      <link rel="stylesheet"
       href="https://maxcdn.bootstrapcdn.com/
       bootstrap/3.3.7/css/bootstrap.min.css">
      <link rel="stylesheet" href="style.css">
```

```
            <!-- JS -->
            <script src="http://openlayers.org/en/v4.3.3/build/ol.js">
            </script>
            <!-- jQuery -->
            <script
             src="https://ajax.googleapis.com/ajax
             /libs/jquery/3.2.1/jquery.min.js"></script>
            <script
             src="http://www.appelsiini.net/download/
              jquery.jeditable.mini.js"></script>
            <!-- Bootstrap -->
            <script src="https://maxcdn.bootstrapcdn.com/bootstrap
             /3.3.7/js/bootstrap.min.js"></script>
    </head>
    <body>
    <!-- Show the map -->
    <div id="map" class="map"></div>
    <!-- Message box to enter message -->
    <div id="message-box"></div>
    <script src="map.js"></script>
    </body>
</html>
```

CSS

The styling of our HTML is written in `style.css`:

```
.message-box {
  min-width: 250px;
}
```

JavaScript

Let's understand our JavaScript `map.js` in steps before jumping to the complete script.

Rendering the map

The `ol` is the `OpenLayers` package that provides the API to play with the maps overlay.

ol.Maps

The core essential component of the `ol` package is `ol.Maps`. It is used to render the maps on the `target` div, which in our case is `map-overlay` a `div` tag from `index.html` where the map will be shown:

```
// Renders the map on the target div
var map = new ol.Map({target: "map"})
```

ol.View

This is used to manage or configure the viewing properties of the map such as zoom level, default center position, and the projection of the map:

```
// To configure center, zoom level and projection of the map
var view = new ol.View({
  zoom: 9
});
```

ol.layer

A layer is a visual representation of data from a source. It is used to show the data on the map that is fetched from remote sources.

It has three basic types of layers:

- `ol.layer.Tile`: This is for layer sources that provide pre-rendered, tiled images in grids that are organized by zoom levels for specific resolutions
- `ol.layer.Image`: This is for server rendered images
- `ol.layer.Vector`: This is for vector data that is rendered client-side

Layers are set when configuring the map object:

```
layers: [
  new ol.layer.Tile(...)
],
```

ol.source

This is used to set the source of the remote data for the layer:

```
layers: [
  new ol.layer.Tile({source: new ol.source.OSM()})
]
```

Plotting messages on the map

We get all the messages based on the extent.

ol.source.Vector

This is used to provide a feature source for the layers. In simple terms, it is used to add a marker on the map.
It has the following options:

- `loader`: This is used to load features like from a remote source. In our case, we are fetching from a remote source using AJAX.
- `strategy`: This is used to set the strategy to load the features. Default uses `ol.loadingstrategy.all`, which loads all the features at once.

ol.Feature

A vector object representing the geographic features with a geometry and other attribute properties. It usually has a single geometry property, which in our case is used to add a marker to the specified coordinates using `ol.geom.Point`, which holds the co-ordinate:

```
/* Show messages on the Map */

var vectorSource = new ol.source.Vector({
  loader: function (extent, resolution, projection) {
    var url = '/message/bbox/' + extent[0] + "," + extent[1] + ","
      + extent[2] + "," + extent[3];
  // Get all the messages from the server based upon the extent
    $.ajax({
      url: url,
        dataType: 'json',
        success: function (response) {
          if (response.error) {
            alert(response.error.message);
          } else {
              // Plot message icon on the map
              $.each(response, function (index, value) {
                var feature = new ol.Feature({
                  geometry: new
                   ol.geom.Point(value.location.coordinates),
                    content: value.content
                });
              vectorSource.addFeature(feature);
              });
          }
      }
    });
```

```
    },
    strategy: ol.loadingstrategy.tile(ol.tilegrid.createXYZ({
      tileSize: 512
    }))
  });
```

We plot on the map by adding a layer of vector and setting the source of this vector data to our previous `vectorSource` where we actually fetch the messages from the backend:

```
// Styling the vector to message icon
var vector = new ol.layer.Vector({
  source: vectorSource,
    style: new ol.style.Style({image: new ol.style.Icon({src:
    "message-box.png", scale: 0.5})})
});
map.addLayer(vector);
```

Listening to message saved events

Storing the message in the database takes some amount of time and we want to update the UI or reflect the state of the UI after the message is successfully saved into the database. We specify an `EventSource` and add an `EventListener` to receive the callback when a new message is stored in the database.

When a new message is saved into the database the `callback function` of the event listener is called and we then plot the message on the map using `ol.Feature`:

```
/* Reactive: Event listener to get updates when new message is
 saved */

var source = new EventSource("/message/subscribe");

// Callback function called on event update
source.addEventListener('message', function (e) {
  var message = $.parseJSON(e.data);
  var feature = new ol.Feature({
    geometry: new ol.geom.Point(message.location.coordinates),
     content: message.content
  });
  vectorSource.addFeature(feature);
}, false);
```

Complete JavaScript

Here is the complete JavaScript with all bits and pieces together:

```
/* Configure Map */
// To configure center, zoom level and projection of the map
var view = new ol.View({
  zoom: 9
});

// Renders the map on the target div
var map = new ol.Map({
// The target div to render map
target: "map",
// Visual representation of data from source
layers: [
  new ol.layer.Tile({source: new ol.source.OSM()})
],
 controls: ol.control.defaults({
   attributionOptions: ({
     collapsible: false
   })
 }),
view: view
});

/* Location  */

var geolocation = new ol.Geolocation({
  projection: view.getProjection()
});
geolocation.on("error", function (error) {
  alert(error.message);
});
// Set styling
var positionFeature = new ol.Feature();
positionFeature.setStyle(new ol.style.Style({
  image: new ol.style.Icon({src: "user.png", scale: 0.5})
}));
// On location change
var centerDefined = false;
geolocation.on("change:position", function () {
  var coordinates = geolocation.getPosition();
  if (!centerDefined) {
    view.setCenter(coordinates);
    centerDefined = true;
  }
  positionFeature.setGeometry(coordinates ? new
```

```
      ol.geom.Point(coordinates) : null);
});

new ol.layer.Vector({
  map: map, source: new ol.source.Vector({
    features: [positionFeature]
  })
});
geolocation.setTracking(true);

/* Message Box */

var element = document.getElementById('message-box');

// Show message box on top of map
var message_box = new ol.Overlay({
  element: element,
   positioning: 'bottom-center'
});
map.addOverlay(message_box);

// Open the message box on clicking on map
map.on('click', function (evt) {
  var coordinate = evt.coordinate;
  var feature = map.forEachFeatureAtPixel(evt.pixel,
   function (feature) {
     return feature;
   });

$(element).popover('destroy');
if (feature) {
  message_box.setPosition(coordinate);
  $(element).popover({
    'placement': 'top',
     'html': true,
     'content': feature.get('content'),
     'animation': false
  });
  $(element).popover('show');
} else {
   message_box.setPosition(coordinate);
   $(element).popover({
     'placement': 'top',
      'html': true,
      'title': "New message",
      'animation': false
   }).data('bs.popover').tip().width(250).height(300)
    .append("<div id='message' style='height:70%'/>");
```

```
      $(element).popover('show');

      // Make the message box editable
      $("#message").editable(function (value, settings) {
        // Save the message at back-end
        $.ajax({
          method: "POST",
           url: "/message",
           data: JSON.stringify({
             content: value,
             location: {
               type: "Point",
                coordinates: [coordinate[0], coordinate[1]]
             }
           }),
            contentType: "application/json; charset=utf-8",
             dataType: "json"
        });
         message_box.setPosition(undefined);
         return value;
      }, {
         type: "textarea",
          submit: "Save"
         });
    }
});


/* Show messages on the Map */

var vectorSource = new ol.source.Vector({
  loader: function (extent, resolution, projection) {
    var url = '/message/bbox/' + extent[0] + "," + extent[1] + ","
      + extent[2] + "," + extent[3];
    // Get all the messages from the server based upon the extent
    $.ajax({
      url: url,
      dataType: 'json',
      success: function (response) {
        if (response.error) {
          alert(response.error.message);
        } else {
            // Plot message icon on the map
            $.each(response, function (index, value) {
              var feature = new ol.Feature({
                geometry: new
                 ol.geom.Point(value.location.coordinates),
                  content: value.content
              });
```

```
                    vectorSource.addFeature(feature);
             });
          }
       }
    });
},
strategy: ol.loadingstrategy.tile(ol.tilegrid.createXYZ({
   tileSize: 512
}))
});

// Styling the vector to message icon
var vector = new ol.layer.Vector({
   source: vectorSource,
   style: new ol.style.Style({image: new ol.style.Icon({
      src: "message-box.png", scale: 0.5})})
   });
map.addLayer(vector);

/* Reactive: Event listener to get updates when new message is
 saved */

var source = new EventSource("/message/subscribe");

source.addEventListener('message', function (e) {
   var message = $.parseJSON(e.data);
   var feature = new ol.Feature({
      geometry: new ol.geom.Point(message.location.coordinates),
       content: message.content,
       author: message.author
   });
   vectorSource.addFeature(feature);
}, false);
```

Application class

We define our `SpringApplication` class to launch our Spring Boot application from the Kotlin code. It reads the application configuration from `application.yml` in our case, but supports being read from various sources.

We use `@SpringBootApplication` to launch our application as a Spring Boot application and `@EnableTransactionManagement` to enable database transaction support for databases:

```
/**
  * To launch Spring Boot application and hold the application
    level properties
  */
@SpringBootApplication
@EnableTransactionManagement
class Application {

  /**
    * To deserialize-serialize the PostGIS data structures
    */
  @Bean
  fun objectMapper(): ObjectMapper =
   Jackson2ObjectMapperBuilder()
   .modulesToInstall(PostGISModule())
   .serializationInclusion(JsonInclude.Include.NON_NULL)
   .build()

  /**
    * Configuring transaction support
    */
  @Bean
  fun transactionManager(@Qualifier("dataSource") dataSource:
   DataSource) = SpringTransactionManager(dataSource)

  /**
    * Initialize our web app each time it runs
    */
  @Bean
  fun init(mr: MessageRepository) = CommandLineRunner {
    mr.createTable()
    mr.deleteAll()
  }
}

/**
  * Launch the Spring Boot application
  */
fun main(args: Array<String>) {
  SpringApplication.run(Application::class.java, *args)
}
```

To configure transaction support with the database we simply need to specify the `@EnableTransactionManagement` annotation and pass `PlatformTransactionManager` with the `transactionManager` bean using the `Application` class:

```
@Bean
fun transactionManager(@Qualifier("dataSource") dataSource:
 DataSource) = SpringTransactionManager(dataSource)
```

Moreover, we need to configure our `object mapper` (`Jackson`) with an additional module for mapping PostGIS data structures:

```
@Bean
fun objectMapper(): ObjectMapper =
 Jackson2ObjectMapperBuilder()
 .modulesToInstall(PostGISModule())
 .serializationInclusion(JsonInclude.Include.NON_NULL)
 .build()
```

You can specify your `main` function for JVM outside the `Application` class, such functions that are not part of any class are called *Top-level functions* in Kotlin and they come from the functional side of Kotlin.

Backend

Let's write some Kotlin code based on the frontend.

Application configuration

`SpringApplication` will load properties from the `application.yml` file and add them to the Spring Environment.

Let's specify properties for our Spring application in the `application.yml` file:

```
logging:
  level:
    org.springframework.web.servlet: INFO
spring:
  datasource:
    platform: "postgis"
    driver-class-name: "org.postgis.DriverWrapper"
    url: "jdbc:postgresql_postGIS://localhost/geo"
    username: "postgres"
```

```
    password: "root"
  mvc:
      async:
        request-timeout: 1000000
```

`Tasync` request timeout is crucial because saving the message into the database takes time and the process is asynchronous and an event is triggered when it is saved. Here the response takes more time than normal to get back, hence we increase the request timeout.

The data-source properties (database) point to our PostGIS database:

```
url: "jdbc:postgresql_postGIS://localhost/YOUR_DATABASE_NAME"
```

 Make sure to change `YOUR_DATABASE_NAME` to the name of your PostGIS database, also change the username and password based on your database credentials.

Data classes

Each time we create a model class, we end up writing the same boilerplate code for:

- Constructor
- Getter-Setter (s)
- `hashCode()`
- `equals()`
- `toString()`

Kotlin introduced the `data` keyword where the compiler automatically derives the following stuff based upon the parameters of the primary constructor:

- Getter-Setter (s), which are not technically due to `data` keywords
- `equals()`/`hashCode()` pair
- `toString()`
- `componentN()` functions corresponding to the properties in their order of declaration
- `copy()` function

It saves a lot of boilerplate code and makes the model classes look clean and concise.

The `Message` class is the data structure representing the messages left by a user on the map. It holds the actual message left, the author of the message and location (coordinates) of the message on the map:

```
/**
 * It represents the message shown on the maps
 */
data class Message(
// The message
var content: String,
// Location of the message
var location: Point? = null,
var id: Int? = null
)
```

Exposed integration

Let's integrate the Exposed library into our application as an ORM for the database layer.

Exposed objects

The `Messages` object provides the mapping between the object and the database and it represents the structure of the table. It is required by the Exposed library:

```
/**
 * Message table structure
 */
object Messages : Table() {
  val id = integer("id").autoIncrement().primaryKey()
  val content = text("content")
  val location = point("location").nullable()
}
```

The following is a diagram of the `Message` class and the `Messages` object required for the Exposed library:

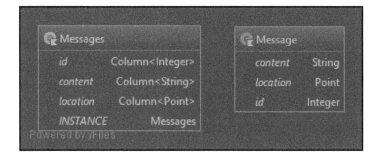

We have specified our `Messages` object for Exposed in the `Database.kt` file. It is recommended to specify all your Exposed objects in a single Kotlin file for easier maintenance.

Extras for geospatial support

Unfortunately, Exposed doesn't natively support PostGIS functionality such as geometry types or geospatial requests. This is an excellent opportunity to use Extension functions by Kotlin and fill the missing support without modifying the original source.

Adding support for location

The location data for the message is in the form of coordinates. To store such a data structure in the database, we define `PointColumnType` to store and get the location data for the message:

```kotlin
 * It represents the point column type for Exposed
 */
class PointColumnType(private val srid: Int = 4326) : ColumnType()
{
  override fun sqlType() = "GEOMETRY(Point, $srid)"
  override fun valueFromDB(value: Any) = if (value is PGgeometry)
   value.geometry else value
  override fun notNullValueToDB(value: Any): Any {
    if (value is Point) {
       if (value.srid == Point.UNKNOWN_SRID) value.srid = srid
       return PGgeometry(value)
    }
  return value
  }
}
```

And add an `Extension` function to directly use `Point Column` in our `Messages` object:

```
/**
 * Extension function to get point column type from the table
 */
fun Table.point(name: String, srid: Int = 4326): Column<Point>
   = registerColumn(name, PointColumnType())
```

Adding support for location-bound queries

One more extra geospatial functionality we need is firing SQL queries within a selected area of the map; that is a bounded box. For that we need to create an expression for the required column type, `PGbox2d`, which represents the bounded location:

```
/**
 * Special type to represent the box and if location of message
 * is inside the specified box
 */
class WithinOp(private val expr1: Expression<*>, private val box:
 PGbox2d) : Op<Boolean>() {
    override fun toSQL(queryBuilder: QueryBuilder) =
      "${expr1.toSQL(queryBuilder)} && ST_MakeEnvelope(${box.llb.x},
      ${box.llb.y}, ${box.urt.x}, ${box.urt.y}, 4326)"
  }
```

And an Extension function to use the feature to check if the message is in the specified region:

```
/**
 * To check if the message location is within the specified box
   area.
 * Returns true if yes else false
 */
infix fun ExpressionWithColumnType<*>.within(box: PGbox2d):
 Op<Boolean>= WithinOp(this, box)
```

Service/Controller

The `MessageController` handles all the URLs, or you can say operations, related to messages. To have a separation of concern in our code. The actual job of saving the message, that is the database operations, is delegated to the respective `Repository` class (`MessageRepository`):

```
/**
 * Exposes the operations related to creating and showing
 * messages through URLs using REST
```

```
    */
@RestController
@RequestMapping("/message")
class MessageController(val repository: MessageRepository) {

  val broadcaster = ReactiveBroadcaster()

/**
  * Creates new message and saves it into DB
  */
@PostMapping
@ResponseStatus(CREATED)
fun create(@RequestBody message: Message): Message {
  val msg = repository.insert(message)
  broadcaster.send(msg)
  return msg
}

/**
  * Get list of all the messages
  */
@GetMapping
fun list() = repository.findAll()

/**
  * Get list of messages in the given bounds
  */
@GetMapping("/bbox/{xMin},{yMin},{xMax},{yMax}")
fun findByBoundingBox(@PathVariable xMin: Double, @PathVariable
 yMin: Double,
 @PathVariable xMax: Double, @PathVariable
 yMax: Double)
 = repository.findByBoundingBox(PGbox2d(Point(xMin, yMin),
 Point(xMax, yMax)))

    /**
      * Subscribes to receive the updates regarding the messages
      */
@GetMapping("/subscribe")
fun subscribe()= broadcaster.subscribe()
}
```

 @GetMapping and @PostMapping annotations are just method-specific shortcuts for @RequestMapping annotations available since Spring Framework 4.3.

Repository

The repository pattern is used to create a layer between database operations and our business logic. It is one popular pattern used to create enterprise level applications. It restricts us to directly performing operations on the database and helps us to test the code.

The following is the hierarchy of `MessageRepository`, which handles the operations to the database:

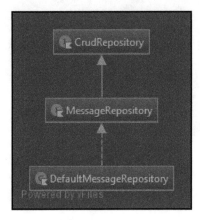

CrudRepository

This defines the structure of the functions for performing create, read, update, and delete operations on the table, including functions exclusively related to geospatial nature:

```
/**
 * Basic CRUD operations related to Geospatial
 */
interface CrudRepository<T, K> {
/**
 * Creates the table
 */
fun createTable()

/**
 * Insert the item
 */
fun insert(t: T): T

/**
 * Get list of all the items
 */
```

```
fun findAll(): Iterable<T>

/**
 * Delete all the items
 */
fun deleteAll(): Int

/**
 * Get list of items in the specified box
 */
fun findByBoundingBox(box: PGbox2d): Iterable<T>

/**
 * Update the location of the user
 */
fun updateLocation(userName: K, location: Point)
}
```

The `MessageRepository` handles the actual interaction with the database; in our case, it performs the CRUD operations on the `Messages` table:

```
/**
 * @inheritDoc
 */
interface MessageRepository: CrudRepository<Message, Int>

/**
 * @inheritDoc
 */
@Repository
@Transactional
class DefaultMessageRepository : MessageRepository {

  /**
   * @inheritDoc
   */
  override fun createTable() = SchemaUtils.create(Messages)

  /**
   * @inheritDoc
   */
  override fun insert(t: Message): Message {
    t.id = Messages.insert(insertQuery(t))[Messages.id]
    return t
  }

  /**
   * @inheritDoc
```

Geospatial Messenger – Spring Boot

```
    */
    override fun findAll() = Messages.selectAll().map {
      it.getMessage() }

    /**
     * @inheritDoc
     */
    override fun findByBoundingBox(box: PGbox2d) = Messages.select {
      Messages.location within box }.map { it.getMessage() }

    /**
     * @inheritDoc
     */
    override fun updateLocation(id:Int, location: Point) {
      location.srid = 4326
      Messages.update({ Messages.id eq id}) { it[Messages.location]
      = location}
    }

    /**
     * @inheritDoc
     */
    override fun deleteAll() = Messages.deleteAll()

}
```

There are lots of advantages of using the Repository pattern. We recommend you read more about it.

Event broadcaster

The `ReactiveBroadcaster` class is an event broadcaster that handles the responsibility of subscribing the observers and sending the updates to interested observers asynchronously and will also do the cleanup after the completion of the events:

```
/**
 * Handles the event broadcasting to the observers in an
 * asynchronous way.
 */
class ReactiveBroadcaster {

  /**
     * Set of emitters for multiple events
```

[54]

```
        */
    private var emitters = synchronizedSet(HashSet<SseEmitter>())

    /**
     * Subscribe to the event
     */
    fun subscribe(): SseEmitter {
      val sseEmitter = SseEmitter()
      // Stop observing the event on completion
      sseEmitter.onCompletion(
      {this.emitters.remove(sseEmitter)
      })
      this.emitters.add(sseEmitter)
      return sseEmitter
      }

    /**
     * Trigger the event update to the observers
     */
    fun send(o: Any) {
      synchronized(emitters) {
        emitters.iterator().forEach {
          try {
            it.send(o, MediaType.APPLICATION_JSON)
          } catch (e: IOException) {}
        }
      }
    }
  }
```

Extension functions

The common and utility functions are grouped in a file named `Extension.kt` (you can specify any name you want). It contains top-level functions that can be used anywhere in the project.

Complete the `Extension.kt` file:

```
/**
 * Builds the insert query for the specified message
 */
fun insertQuery(m: Message): Messages.(UpdateBuilder<*>) -> Unit =
{
  if (m.id != null) it[id] = m.id
  it[content] = m.content
  it[location] = m.location
```

```
    }

    /**
     * Create the message object from Result row
     * @return message
     */
    fun ResultRow.getMessage() =
      Message(this[Messages.content], this[Messages.location],
      this[Messages.id])

    // Other extension functions
```

Testing

To test our Spring Boot application we need to test the URLs we are handling in our `Controller`, which means we need to write a test class for each `Controller`.

Gradle dependency

We need to add the following dependencies to our `build.gradle` file for testing:

```
    // Testing
    testCompile group: 'junit', name: 'junit', version: '4.12'
    testCompile "org.springframework.boot:spring-boot-starter-test"
```

Test cases

All the tests are put in the `test` module with the same package name of the code. Mainly the test cases are written for the `Controller`, but you can even write for `Repository` for which you'll need to mock the database using `Mockito` or some other mocking library.

The `MockMvc` class is the entry point for performing server-side tests. We can perform HTTP requests such as `GET`, `POST`, and others on the URLs to test the REST endpoints.

`MessageControllerTests`: Test cases for the `MessageController` are written in human readable names using ` while writing function names.

Consider the following example:

```kotlin
@RunWith(SpringRunner::class)
@SpringBootTest
class MessageControllerTests {

  @Autowired lateinit var context: WebApplicationContext
  @Autowired lateinit var messageRepository: MessageRepository
  @Autowired lateinit var mapper: ObjectMapper

  /**
   * Entry point to server side tests
   */
  lateinit var mockMvc: MockMvc

  @Before
  fun setup() {
    messageRepository.deleteAll()
    mockMvc = webAppContextSetup(this.context).build()
  }

  @Test
  fun `Create new message`() {
    val message = Message("""We have some dummy message over here
      to perform some testing and I have started to write test
      cases for my code""".trimMargin()
      , Point(0.0, 0.0))
    mockMvc.perform(post("/message")
    .content(mapper.writeValueAsString(message))
    .contentType(APPLICATION_JSON_UTF8))
    .andExpect(status().isCreated)
  }

  @Test
  fun `Get all messages`() {
    messageRepository.insert(Message("I love Kotlin"))
    messageRepository.insert(Message("I love this book",
    Point(0.0, 0.0)))
    mockMvc.perform(get("/message")
    .accept(APPLICATION_JSON_UTF8)).andExpect(status().isOk)
  }

  @Test
  fun `Find messages in the specified region`() {
    messageRepository.insert(Message("I love Kotlin", Point(0.0,
    0.0)))
    messageRepository.insert(Message("I love this book",
    Point(1.0, 1.0)))
```

```
        mockMvc.perform(get("/message/bbox/{xMin},{yMin},{xMax},
        {yMax}", -1, -1, 2, 2)
        .accept(APPLICATION_JSON_UTF8))
        .andExpect(status().isOk)
    }

    @Test
    fun `Subscribe to the message`() {
      mockMvc.perform(get("/message/subscribe"))
        .andExpect(status().isOk)
    }

}
```

Pro-tips

If you're still struggling with some issues while building Spring Boot applications, here are some pro-tips to help you build faster and better Spring Boot+Kotlin applications.

All-open compiler plugin

By default, classes and the functions in Kotlin are final. In order to make a particular class or function non-final you need to use the `open` keyword. It is one of the pain points of using Kotlin with Spring as the classes for external configuration properties (Spring beans proxified with CGLIB like `@Configuration` classes) are required to be `open`.

Fortunately, with Kotlin v1.0.6, there is a Kotlin-Spring plugin that tells the compiler to `open` classes and their member functions for classes annotated or meta-annotated with one of the following annotations:

- `@Component`
- `@Async`
- `@Transactional`
- `@Cacheable`
- Also, classes annotated with `@Configuration`, `@Controller`, `@RestController`, `@Service`, or `@Repository` are automatically opened since these annotations are meta-annotated with `@Component`

In a nutshell, it becomes much easier to `open` the required configuration classes by using Spring.

Spring starter

Spring Initializr is a cool tool by Spring Team to easily bootstrap your application with all the starter code and required dependencies. It helps to create a project instantly. You can even create the project with Kotlin support.

It's available at `https://start.spring.io/`.

Playing with the Java to Kotlin converter

The Java to Kotlin converter in IntelliJ IDEA (**Menu** | **Code** | **Convert Java File to Kotlin File** or *Ctrl* + *Alt* + *Shift* + *K* in Windows) is quite a handy tool to quickly convert your Java code to Kotlin. It's not a 100% solid conversion, but it's good enough, hence it's recommended to review the code after converting.

Migrating to Kotlin

Already have an existing application written in Java and curious how to migrate it to Kotlin? Don't worry, the following tips have you covered.

Should I rewrite the existing Java code in Kotlin?

If your existing codebase or application is already in Java then kindly *don't rewrite* the existing code in Kotlin, instead, you can start by writing tests for your existing application in Kotlin that way you get comfortable writing Kotlin and get test cases for your application (which you probably haven't written yet).

Later you can write the new functionalities in Kotlin (thanks to the excellent inter-operability with Java).

What if I want to rewrite Java to Kotlin?

Well, you can if you really want. I'd recommend not converting everything to Kotlin and just convert the Java files that you touch while implementing some features or fixing some bugs.

Summary

You might have noticed how Kotlin cuts down the boilerplate code and helps you write clean and concise code. It even makes the whole app development easier and fun. Overall, Kotlin is a great language with excellent IDE support and it has a light-weight runtime, which is a bonus considering the fact that it comes with 100% interoperability with Java. The Null safety helps to handle all the `nulls` at compile time and saves us from making a Billion-Dollar Mistake (`https://en.wikipedia.org/wiki/Tony_Hoare`).

We have successfully built our production ready geospatial messenger, which you can use to leave messages on the map on particular co-ordinates with Spring Boot while leveraging amazing features of Kotlin. We also saw how to write test cases in Kotlin, which is a great way to start writing Kotlin code in case you're afraid of writing actual logic.

In the next chapter, we will look at how to build web applications (RESTful web services) with the Ktor framework, which is built with Kotlin in mind and is a great alternative to Spring Boot when building web applications in Kotlin.

3
Social Media Aggregator Android App

We have seen the power of Kotlin for Spring Boot. However, building a mobile application is different. It's much more compact compared to browser apps, they have to be delivered fast. It has to be 10 times faster in terms of processing user input.

Kotlin's features along with its compiler's support for the Android app development makes developing Android apps much easier, interesting, and productive. The biggest advantage of using Kotlin is its *Null Safety* feature. `NullPointerException` is the foe for any Android apps and is a nightmare for developers. Kotlin simply kills the possibility of `NullPointerException`. It also has a robust API also. Apart from Null Safety Kotlin has features such as extension function, Lambdas, delegated properties, and functions such as `let`, `apply`, `with`, and `when`. All this makes Android app development so much fun. The Kotlin team have built an Anko library, which is also loaded with lots of features. Anko is one more reason to love Kotlin.

Kotlin is a great language and the best way to learn any language is by gaining practical knowledge. In this chapter, you will learn to create a social media aggregator app along with Kotlin's features. You will learn to apply Kotlin in the Android way.

In this chapter, you will learn:

- How to start an activity
- Dealing with preferences
- Model classes
- `RecyclerView`, adapters, and click events
- String interpolation
- Functions such as `let`, `apply`, `with`, `when`, and so on

We will be referencing classes and files we have created for the companion app. Make sure while reading you have the source code handy.

Setting up Kotlin

We need Android Studio for Android application development. Initially, we were using Eclipse and the Android team was providing good support with ADT release, but now it's better that we have moved to Android Studio, which has been developed by IntelliJ IDEA. We should quickly cover the development environment-related information here. The installation is straightforward. Please refer to Android's developer website: `https://developer.android.com/studio/install.html` for any setup and installation related help.

Android Studio 3.0 has come up recently and has built-in support for Kotlin. We recommend using that now. And those who have Android Studio 2.3 or lower need the Kotlin plugin setup. You can find all the relevant information at `https://kotlinlang.org/docs/tutorials/kotlin-android.html`.

Setting up the Kotlin plugin for Android Studio

In order to ensure that Android Studio supports Kotlin, the first thing to do is to install the Kotlin plugin for Android Studio by clicking on **Android Studio** | **Preferences** | **Plugins** | **Browse Repository** |, type `Kotlin` in the search box, and install:

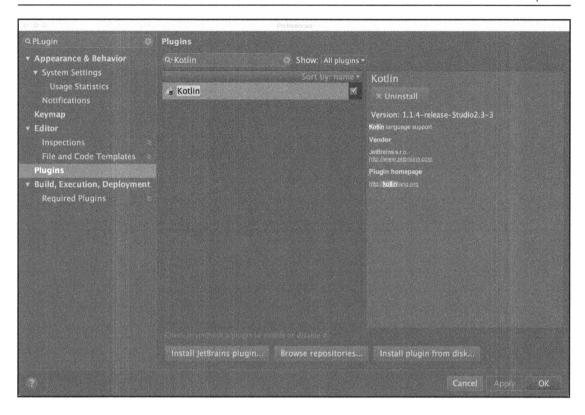

Android Studio will ask for a restart. Please follow the steps. The next step will be adding Kotlin classpath to the project level `build.gradle` file:

```
1   // Top-level build file where you can add configuration options common to all sub-pro
2
3   buildscript {
4       ext.kotlin_version = '1.1.4-3'
5       ext.anko_version = '0.10.0'
6       repositories {
7           jcenter()
8       }
9       dependencies {
10          classpath 'com.android.tools.build:gradle:2.3.3'
11          classpath "org.jetbrains.kotlin:kotlin-gradle-plugin:$kotlin_version"
12
13          // NOTE: Do not place your application dependencies here; they belong
14          // in the individual module build.gradle files
15      }
16  }
```

Once the classpath is added we will add Gradle project dependency into the app level `build.gradle` and apply the Kotlin plugin:

```
apply plugin: 'com.android.application'
apply plugin: 'kotlin-android'
apply plugin: 'kotlin-android-extensions'
```

Now, add the Kotlin (the following screenshot also shows Anko, you can skip this for now) dependencies in the app level `build.gradle` file:

```
compile "org.jetbrains.kotlin:kotlin-stdlib-jre7:$kotlin_version"
compile "org.jetbrains.anko:anko:$anko_version"
```

We are using Kotlin version 1.1.4. Sync your Gradle project and setup is complete!

Here are some tips that will save you time during set up. Always follow official tutorials. Check if your studio has the proper version. In the plugin, setup steps make a note of enabling plugin support by writing the apply plugin: `kotlin-android` in the `build.gradle` file. And make sure you restart the studio once all installation is complete.

Getting started

We assume that you are already aware of the basics of Android, which includes project creation, Gradle sync, and so on. Once you create a project you usually land up in the IDE where you can see the `MainActivity.java` in front of you. Now targeting an entire project to be developed in Kotlin you should start converting this Java activity to Kotlin activity. Brilliant Android Studio comes to the help of the developer right from the beginning. It has a shortcut that you can use to convert your Java activity into Kotlin activity very easily.

Converting Java code to Kotlin code

From the menu select **Code | Convert Java File to Kotlin File** and kaboom! Your task is done. Your first Kotlin activity is ready. As a means of verifying everything is fine, we suggest you run the project once. If you can see **Hello World** on the emulator or device that means you have successfully configured Kotlin for Android.

Or, create a new Kotlin file (**File** | **New** | **Kotlin File/Class**), and then paste your Java code into that file, when prompted, click **Yes** to convert the code to Kotlin. You can check **Don't show this dialog next time**, which makes it easy to dump Java code snippets into your Kotlin files:

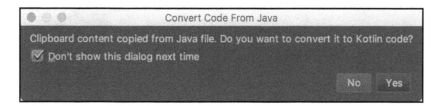

 Have a watchful eye on such conversion that IDE is doing for you. *With great power comes great responsibility.* It's always better to check whether IDE has done the right thing for you or not. IDE is not yet that smart and stable that it can convert the code with optimization as well.

Creating a social media aggregator

You will build an app that may look like the following:

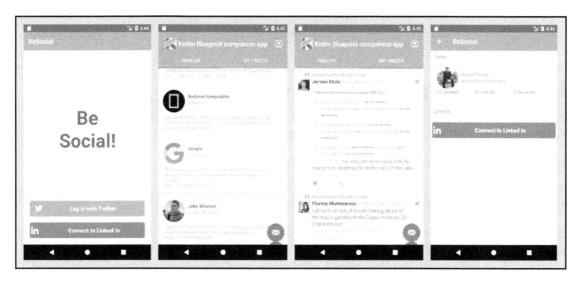

UI representation of social media aggregator

And an application directory that will look like the following:

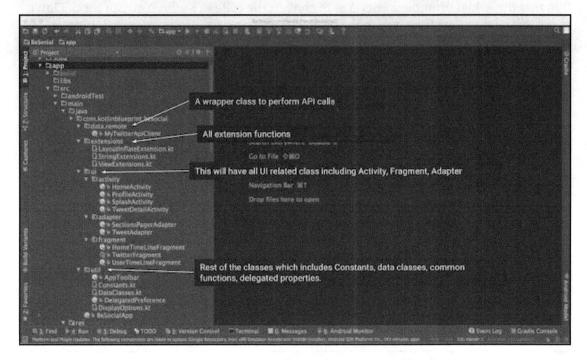

Application directory

Using datatypes and conversion

In Kotlin, everything is an object. Kotlin has pretty much the same number of related data types compared to Java. But they are not exactly the same.

In Java, the following is true:

```
int num=10;
double bigNum=num;
```

But in Kotlin if you try to do such a thing it will give a compile-time error. This means implicit widening is not allowed in Kotlin. However, the main thing we want to discuss in this section is, with every number type Kotlin supports some explicit conversion and that can fill the gap of not having an implicit widening feature. Also, we often use utility methods from Java wrapper classes such as `Integer.parseInt()`, `Float.valueOf()`, and so on.

Every number type supports the following conversions:

`toByte()`	**Byte**
`toShort()`	Short
`toInt()`	Int
`toLong()`	Long
`toFloat()`	Float
`toDouble()`	Double
`toChar()`	Char

Let's say a class is expecting the `int` value and you have the `float` value as a parameter, you can use `toInt()` and get the job done. No casting is required:

```
RoundedBitmapDisplayer(someFloatValue.toInt())
```

String interpolation

A string is a most commonly and heavily used class. String literal is also an instance of the string class. String interpolation has the most beautiful features in Kotlin.

Interpolation is basically smart string concatenation. A typical string concatenation can look as follows:

```
val name="Kotlin Blueprints"
println("Name $name")
```

In Android, there can be many cases where we do string concatenation and string interpolation can help us.

Remember! We have to display dynamic labels on `TextView` countless times in the app. The code for that using string interpolation can look as follows:

```
txtFollowers.text = "$followersCount
  ${getString(R.string.cnt_followers)}"
txtFriendsCount.text = "$friendsCount
  ${getString(R.string.cnt_friends)}"
txtTweets.text = "${status.retweetCount}
  ${getString(R.string.cnt_retweet)}"
```

If you observe the preceding code snippet, we actually use both objects and properties as well.

 String interpolation internally uses the `StringBuilder` class to achieve this. Also, we observed that there is no caching performed. Every time the statement executes a new object gets created. Let's hope that Kotlin will fix this soon in coming versions.

String utility methods

In the world of Java, we know due to null checks how many times we used to check nulls and an empty string as well. Kotlin is aware of this pain point and the stereotype `code.kotlin.text` package has many such useful functions.

`true` is returned if this character sequence is empty (contains no characters):

```
fun CharSequence.isEmpty(): Boolean
```

`true` is returned if this character sequence is not empty and contains some characters except whitespace characters:

```
fun CharSequence.isNotBlank(): Boolean
```

`true` is returned if this character sequence is not empty:

```
fun CharSequence.isNotEmpty(): Boolean
```

`true` is returned if this nullable character sequence is either null or empty or consists solely of whitespace characters:

```
fun CharSequence?.isNullOrBlank(): Boolean
```

`true` is returned if this nullable character sequence is either null or empty:

```
fun CharSequence?.isNullOrEmpty(): Boolean
```

It's a happy moment seeing such functions readily available. We do not need to worry about handling white spaces as a value of `String`.

Classes

Like any other object-oriented programming languages that have classes, Kotlin is no exception. But features of dealing with classes are exceptional. Kotlin classes are different to traditional programming languages. It has a constructor in the class header itself. It has a different way of passing a parameter of a superclass and a lot more.

Constructors

Unlike any other programming languages, Kotlin also has a primary/default and secondary constructor. The primary/default constructor is a part of the class header itself. Consider the following code snippet:

```
class SectionsPagerAdapter(fm: FragmentManager) :
FragmentPagerAdapter(fm)
```

Here see how we pass the object directly to the superclass. No explicit super call is required. For example, `super(someParam)`, no such code is required.

The problem with this approach is you cannot access those parameters in the class, that is, `fm` cannot be used in the class. But if you want to use that parameter in the class, Kotlin has a syntax. For that refer to our other class `TweetAdapter`. There we want to use items and the `callback` methods inside the class, so we used `val`:

```
class TweetAdapter(val items: List<Tweet>,
 val callback: (Tweet) ->
 Unit) : RecyclerView.Adapter<TweetAdapter.ViewHolder>() {
   // Class body
 }
```

You cannot perform anything in the primary constructor header section. Kotlin is aware of this and that's why we have the `init` block to do some extra stuff while creating an object.

Initialization code can be placed in *initializer blocks*, which are prefixed with the `init` keyword. The `init` block can look like the following code snippet:

```
class Customer(name: String) {
   init {
     logger.info("Customer initialized with value ${name}")
   }
 }
```

The class can have a secondary constructor as well:

```
class Person {
  constructor(parent: Person) {
    parent.children.add(this)
  }
}
```

What if a class wants to have both a primary and secondary constructor and wants to refer to its own constructor as a part of a constructor chaining concept:

```
class Person(val name: String) {
  constructor(name: String, parent: Person) : this(name) {
    parent.children.add(this)
  }
}
```

Data classes

One of the coolest features in Kotlin is data classes. All pain that we used to take to create and maintain **plain old Java object** (**POJO**) classes in Java is gone. No need to have those dedicated packages to hold your model class. Any Kotlin file can hold your data class. By default it provides you methods such as `toString()`, `equals()`, `copy()`, and `hashCode()` method implementation. In Android, we mostly use this type of class to hold our JSON responses in form of model classes. You can check out data classes we created in `DataClasses.kt`. The following code snippet is an extract of the `DataClasses.kt` file:

```
data class LinkedInUser(val id: String,
 val firstName: String,
 val lastName: String,
 val headline: String,
 val siteStandardProfileRequest:
 StandardProfileRequest)

data class StandardProfileRequest(val url: String)
```

The data classes start with the data keyword. With data classes we need to keep a few things in mind:

- The primary constructor needs to have at least one parameter
- All primary constructor parameters need to be marked as `val` or `var`
- The data classes cannot be `abstract`, `open`, `sealed`, or `inner`
- (before 1.1) The data classes may only implement interfaces

Inheritance

Android loves inheritance. We can see this affection in `Activity`, `Fragments`, `Services`, `Receivers`, and the `Application` class. EVERYWHERE !! And inspired by this we also do it in multiple places. But here comes the twist. In Kotlin all classes are final by default. So if you want some class to be open for the extension you have to use the `open` keyword.

 The open annotation on a class is the opposite of Java's final, that is, it allows others to inherit from this class. By default, all classes in Kotlin are final, which corresponds to *Effective Java, Item 17: Design and document for inheritance or else prohibit it* (`https://books.google.fr/books?id=ka2VUBqHiWkClpg=PA87ots=yZKjLhuZRYpg=PA87#v=onepageqf=false`).

An open class and inheritance example can look as follows:

```
open class Base {
  open fun v() {}
  fun nv() {}
}

class Derived() : Base() {
  override fun v() {}
}
```

Kotlin still holds the `abstract` class and its concept and it's aligned with Java concepts. Take a look at our `abstract` class in the app:

```
/**
 * A simple [Fragment] subclass.
 * Use the [TwitterFragment.newInstance] factory method to
 * create an instance of this fragment.
 */
abstract class TwitterFragment : Fragment() {

  override fun onCreate(savedInstanceState: Bundle?) {
    super.onCreate(savedInstanceState)
  }

  // Inflate the layout for this fragment
  override fun onCreateView(inflater: LayoutInflater?, container:
    ViewGroup?, savedInstanceState: Bundle?): View? =
    inflater?.inflate(R.layout.fragment_twitter, container, false)

  override fun onViewCreated(view: View?, savedInstanceState:
    Bundle?) {
```

```
        loadTimeline()composeTweet.setOnClickListener {
          val builder = TweetComposer.Builder(activity)
          .text("Tweet about #KotlinBluePrint")
          builder.show()
        }
      }

    abstract fun loadTimeline()
    }
```

 In a final class (for example, a class with no *open* annotation), open members are prohibited. And a member marked override is itself open, that is, it may be overridden in subclasses. If you want to prohibit re-overriding, use `final`.

Singletons

Singletons are part of many architecture designs. We like to create the object once and use it multiple times with easy access. Developers like to make DBHelpers and SharedPreferences manager classes singleton. But not all developers know how to create the best singleton class. The best singleton class is that which supports every scenario of multi-threading. A singleton class has various object creation and initialization methods such as eager initialization, lazy initialization, double check, and so on.

A vastly used Java code to achieve singleton design pattern and object initialization will look as follows:

```java
public class Singleton {

  private static Singleton instance = null;

  private Singleton(){
}

  private synchronized static void createInstance() {
    if (instance == null) {
      instance = new Singleton();
    }
  }

  public static Singleton getInstance() {
    if (instance == null) createInstance();
    return instance;
  }
}
```

Kotlin creates a singleton with one keyword, that is, `object`:

```
object Singleton {
  init {
    println("init complete")
  }

  fun doSomeThing() {
    // Body of function goes here
  }
}
```

> Objects never have a constructor. You cannot pass any parameter if you
> want to create a singleton object with some initial value, it's not possible
> the preceding way.

lateinit versus lazy initialization

While programming there is always a situation where we think whether to initialize an
object now or when it's required. Well with Kotlin's `lateinit` and `lazy`, no need to worry.
Often `lateinit` and `lazy` confuses developers, let's understand them better here.

lateinit

As the word says, it indicates that you will initialize before it's the first usage. We cannot
use this property for primitive like classes, for example, `Int`, `Float`, and so on.

You can initialize this type of object in any place where it's accessible. Every non-null object
should be initialized at the time of declaration. But many times it's not possible. What if
objects are getting initialized using **Dependency Injection** (**DI**). Test setup functions are
another place where you want to initialize the object later:

```
class HomeTimeLineFragmentPresenterTest {

  lateinit var mock: TwitterCore

  @SetUp fun setup() {
    mock = // Initialize mock
  }

  @Test fun test() {
    // Perform mock test
```

```
        }
    }
```

lateinit cannot be used with nullable and Java primitive types. If you want your property to be initialized from outside in a way probably unknown beforehand, use lateinit. lateinit will always use var and not val.

The lazy property

The lazy is a very handy feature in Kotlin. We don't initialize any object unless we require it. This is quite an optimized approach. A typical case can be binding on a view with an object when required. We initialized a toolbar in HomeActivity to demonstrate the lazy property. There can be many other use cases using it:

```
val toolbar by lazy { find<Toolbar>(R.id.toolbar) }
```

A lazy delegated property can only be used with val. Whatever you define inside the block that will get executed only once.

Use it carefully, initializing a heavy object when it is required can affect application response. Do not execute functions doing too much inside the lazy block.

Control flow

It is hardly possible that your code does not use control flow somewhere in the project. Control flow is required to drive the flow of your business logic. Kotlin offers the control flows such as loops, conditions, and case base selection, but in a smarter way.

The when() expression

Typically, when replaces the switch case of traditional programming languages such as C, Java, and so on. A simple when block can look as follows:

```
when (x) {
    1 -> print("x == 1")
    2 -> print("x == 2")
    else -> {
        // Note the block  print("x is neither 1 nor 2")
```

```
    }
  }
```

No verbosity and the simplest to understand isn't it! We have used the when block in the
app at multiple places; in the chapter, we will quote one from
the DelegatedPrefernce.kt file. The when() function can be used as an expression or as
a statement. The following is the code we have used in our app:

```
val result: Any = when (defaultValue) {
    is Boolean -> getBoolean(key, defaultValue)
    is Int -> getInt(key, defaultValue)
    is Long -> getLong(key, defaultValue)
    is Float -> getFloat(key, defaultValue)
    is String -> getString(key, defaultValue)
    else -> throw IllegalArgumentException()
}
```

You can also return the result when the function is evaluated, something like the following:

```
return when {
    day > 0 -> "$day d"
    hours > 0 -> "$hours h"
    minute > 0 -> "$minute m"
    else -> "$second s"
}
```

Also, see how we are using it in SectionsPagerAdapter to get the Fragment instance:

```
override fun getItem(position: Int): Fragment = when (position) {
    0 -> HomeTimeLineFragment.newInstance()
    1 -> UserTimeLineFragment.newInstance()
    else -> {
      throw RuntimeException("No next fragments found, check your
        page count and number of fragments instantiated")
    }
}
```

In the preceding code snippet whatever value is returned from the when block will be
available in the result value. And the when block without a return value can look as follows:

```
when (value) {
    is Boolean -> putBoolean(key, value)
    is Int -> putInt(key, value)
    is Long -> putLong(key, value)
    is Float -> putFloat(key, value)
    is String -> putString(key, value)
    else -> throw IllegalArgumentException()
}.apply()
```

when can also be used as a replacement for an if...else chain. If no argument is supplied, the branch conditions are simply Boolean expressions, and a branch is executed when its condition is true. See the following code that explains how the if...else ladder can be replaced with the when function:

```
when {
    x.isOdd() -> print("x is odd")
    x.isEven() -> print("x is even")
    else -> print("x is funny")
}
```

Getters and setters

In Kotlin any class can have a property, basically a member data in Java language. And for property having the getters and setters is optional. If you have any specific behavior or actions to perform while getting or setting the value, then having getters and setters makes sense and it can be performed as shown previously.

Declaring a property

The full syntax for declaring a property is:

```
var <propertyName>[: <PropertyType>] [=
<property_initializer>]
  [<getter>]
  [<setter>]
```

The initialization, getter, and setter for the objects are optional. The property type is optional if it can be inferred from the initializer (or from the getter return type, as shown in the following snippet).

In Java:

```
TwitterSession session =
  TwitterCore.getInstance().getSessionManager().getActiveSession();
```

In Kotlin:

```
TwitterCore.getInstance().sessionManager.activeSession
```

We have defined getter and setter to deal with the toolbar title. Take a look at the
`AppToolbar.kt` interface:

```
var toolbarTitle: String
  get() = toolbar.title.toString()
  set(value) {
    toolbar.title = value
  }
```

The previous `toolbarTitle` is simply accessible in the `setUpToolbar()` function:

```
toolbarTitle=toolbar.context.getString(R.string.toolbar_title)
```

Notice `toolbar.context` as well. This is nothing but property style access to
the `getContext()` function:

```
LayoutInflater.from(this?.context).inflate(layoutId, this,
  attachToRoot)
```

The previous line inside `LayoutInflateExtension.kt` is another example of accessing
context in a property style.

Apart from context, there are many other getters and setters that we have used in a
property style access.

Take a look at `HomeActivity` and how we are passing
a `SupportFragmentManager` instance and how `container.adapter` is replacing
the `setAdapter()` function call:

```
container.adapter = SectionsPagerAdapter(supportFragmentManager)
```

Getting and setting the text from `TextView` also follows the same concept. We have used it
in the `TweetAdapter.kt` class:

```
txtName.text = user.name
txtHandler.text = "@${user.screenName}"
txtTweet.text = text
```

Here is another example. You will find this property style access to loads of places:

```
rvTimeline.layoutManager = LinearLayoutManager(context)
```

Interfaces

Interfaces are very popular among developers. They are used to decouple the code. Kotlin interfaces are very much like Java 8 interfaces. That means they can have both abstract methods as well as method implementation.

You can declare properties in interfaces. A property declared in an interface can either be abstract, or it can provide implementations for accessors. Properties declared in interfaces can't have backing fields and therefore accessors declared in interfaces can't reference them.

Take a look at our interface `AppToolbar.kt`, which deals with the `Toolbar`. It has got a property that provides a title to the `Toolbar` and it has a function that initiates it with required data:

```
interface AppToolbar {
  val toolbar: Toolbar

  var toolbarTitle: String
   get() = toolbar.title.toString()
   set(value) {
     toolbar.title = value
   }

  fun setUpToolbar() {
    toolbarTitle=toolbar.context.getString(R.string.toolbar_title)
    toolbar.setLogo(R.mipmap.ic_launcher)
    toolbar.inflateMenu(R.menu.menu_home)
    toolbar.setOnMenuItemClickListener {
      when (it.itemId) {
        R.id.menuProfile ->
          toolbar.context.startActivity<ProfileActivity>()
      }
      true
    }
  }
}
```

Kotlin Android extension

If you know C# you might be familiar with extension functions. Extension functions allow you to add new functionality to the existing class without inheriting it.

Ditching the findViewById() method

In the world of Android, `findViewById()` is the necessity. And we know how painful it is to code it every time for every view. Yes, a butter knife will give some relief, but it has its own disadvantages (we will not go into them). Since Kotlin is targeting for Android app development, it has to provide the solution to this problem. And Kotlin's `kotlin-android-extensions` is the solution.

If the following is your view:

```
<com.twitter.sdk.android.core.identity.TwitterLoginButton
  android:id="@+id/loginWithTwitter"
  android:layout_width="wrap_content"
  android:layout_height="wrap_content" />
```

A typical Java code would look as follows:

```
TwitterLoginButton loginWithTwitter = (TwitterLoginButton)
 findViewById(R.id.loginWithTwitter);
loginWithTwitter.setOnClickListener( new OnClickListener() {
  @Override public void onClick(View v) {
    // TODO Auto-generated method stub
  }
});
```

But with Kotlin it's one import statement and we are done:

```
import kotlinx.android.synthetic.main.activity_main.*

composeTweet.setOnClickListener {
  // TODO Auto-generated method stub***Do what you want with the
   click here***
}
```

To achieve this we need to add `apply plugin:kotlin-android-extensions` in our app level `build.gradle` file.

View extensions

Often we need to play with the view's visibility. Extension functions can help us here. If you see in the `ViewExtensions.kt` file, there are two extension functions written inside:

```
fun View.visible() {
  this.visibility = View.VISIBLE
}
```

```
fun View.gone() {
    this.visibility = View.GONE
}
```

So now suppose you want to change the visibility of any of the views, you can write the code in the following way:

```
cardLinkedInUser.visible()
btnLoginLinkedIn.gone()
```

 Extension functions are visible for all child classes as well. For example, we wrote the extension function for the `View` class. So we can call the `visible()` and `gone()` functions from any subclass of `View`, that is `EditText`, `TextView`, `Button`, `CardView`, `RecyclerView`, `ListView`, and so on.

Fragment LayoutInflater extension

If the following is the code in Kotlin for inflating layout for any fragment, do you see any possibility for improvement by applying any kind of extension function?

```
override fun onCreateView(inflater: LayoutInflater?, container:
  ViewGroup?,
  savedInstanceState: Bundle?): View? =
  inflater?.inflate(R.layout.fragment_twitter, container, false)
```

We would advise creating an extension on `ViewGroup`. Let's try it:

```
fun ViewGroup?.inflate(layoutId: Int, attachToRoot: Boolean) =
  LayoutInflater.from(this?.context).inflate(layoutId, this,
  attachToRoot)
```

Three things to highlight. We make the `inflate()` method null safe by adding `ViewGroup?`, we utilize the same object to get the `context` to pass it in two places. Isn't it cool!

Now let's add a default parameter for allowing the user to attach the layout to the root and make this code more delicious. The `final` extension will look like the following code. You can refer it to `LayoutInflateExtension.kt`:

```
fun ViewGroup?.inflate(layoutId: Int, attachToRoot: Boolean =
  false) = LayoutInflater.from(this?.context).inflate(layoutId,
  this, attachToRoot)
```

The extension that we created can be called in the following two ways:

```
// Using default parameter attachToRoot with value false
container.inflate(R.layout.fragment_twitter)


// Passing value true to attachToRoot parameter and overriding
  default value.
container.inflate(R.layout.fragment_twitter,true)
```

The Standard.kt function

Kotlin has already defined some extension functions and `Standard.kt` is part of those functions. It has functions like `with()`, `apply()`, `let()`. The file has more than these extension functions, but we are only highlighting the ones commonly used in Android:

```
**
 * Calls the specified function [block] with the given [receiver]
   as its receiver and returns its result.
 */
@kotlin.internal.InlineOnly
public inline fun <T, R> with(receiver: T, block: T.() -> R): R =
  receiver.block()

/**
  * Calls the specified function [block] with `this` value as its
    receiver and returns `this` value.
  */
@kotlin.internal.InlineOnly
public inline fun <T> T.apply(block: T.() -> Unit): T { block();
  return this }

/**
  * Calls the specified function [block] with `this` value as its
    argument and returns its result.
  */
@kotlin.internal.InlineOnly
public inline fun <T, R> T.let(block: (T) -> R): R = block(this)
```

The with() function

This calls a given function or block of functions on that object and returns the result. For example, while working with `RecyclerView` we always bind our views using `ViewHolder`. The `ViewHolder` always sets the value for its child views.

With the help of POJO, we retrieve value out of POJO and set them on view. For the `TweetAdapter` class the `showData` function can look like the following if the programming language is Java:

```java
public void showData(Tweet tweet) {
   imgProfilePic.setRoundedImageOption
   (tweet.user.getProfileImageUrlHttps());
   txtName.setText(tweet.getUser().getName());
   txtHandler.setText(tweet.getUser().getScreenName());
   txtTweet.setText(tweet.getText());
}
```

Did you notice everywhere we have to use a `tweet` object to get values out of it? Kotlin being a smart language recognizes this problem and solves it with the help of the `with()` function. Kotlin code will look as follows:

```kotlin
fun showData(tweet: Tweet) {
   with(tweet) {
      imgProfilePic.setRoundedImageOption(user.profileImageUrlHttps)
      txtName.text = user.name
      txtHandler.text = "@${user.screenName}"
      txtTweet.text = text
   }
}
```

The apply() function

The `apply()` function simply executes the function or given block with its own reference `this` as the receiver and returns the same updated object.

A typical case of using `apply` can be:

```kotlin
supportActionBar?.apply {
   setDisplayHomeAsUpEnabled(true)
   setDisplayShowHomeEnabled(true)
}
```

Which is as good as writing:

```kotlin
if(supportActionBar != null){
   supportActionBar.setDisplayHomeAsUpEnabled(true);
   supportActionBar.setDisplayShowHomeEnabled(true);
}
```

The let() function

The `let()` function simply executes the function or given block with its own reference `this` as a receiver and returns the result. In Android, you can use it to execute all that code where you put a null check and then try to get and set value over it. We have shown you the use case in `UserTimeLineFrgment.kt`, where the code is as follows:

```
TwitterCore.getInstance().sessionManager.activeSession?.let {
  val userTimeline = UserTimeline.Builder()
    .screenName(TwitterCore.getInstance()
    .sessionManager.activeSession.userName)
    .build()
  val adapter = TweetTimelineRecyclerViewAdapter.Builder(context)
    .setTimeline(userTimeline)
    .setViewStyle(R.style.tw__TweetLightWithActionsStyle)
    .build()
    rvTimeline.layoutManager = LinearLayoutManager(context)
    rvTimeline.adapter = adapter
}
```

Functions in Kotlin

In Kotlin we don't have methods. But we have functions.

Calling a function in Kotlin uses the old traditional approach.

Single-expression function

When your function is doing nothing but simply evaluating the expression and returning a result, you can omit the curly braces. Look at how we are using it in multiple places:

```
override fun getItemCount() = items.size

fun buildScope(): Scope = Scope.build(Scope.R_BASICPROFILE,
  Scope.R_EMAILADDRESS, Scope.W_SHARE)

override fun getCount(): Int = 3 // Show 3 total pages.
```

Inline function

If you paid attention to our previous chapter, you will remember that we discussed `Standard.kt` file and functions. All those functions are inline. Inline function means replacing the body of the function at the time of building the file. It's not an actual function call.

Using higher-order functions (`https://kotlinlang.org/docs/reference/lambdas.html`) imposes certain runtime penalties—each function is an object, and it captures a closure, that is, those variables that are accessed in the body of the function. Memory allocations (both for function objects and classes) and virtual calls introduce runtime overhead.

But it appears that in many cases this kind of overhead can be eliminated by inlining the lambda expressions. The functions shown are good examples of these situations.

Default and named parameters

Do you ever end up writing multiple method overloads to achieve something, just because an existing function requires one extra parameter just to reuse an existing function's logic? Or ever double-check whether the parameter you have passed in a function is binding with a desired method's parameter or not? Yes, Kotlin can solve this problem with default and named parameters.

Default parameter

Often we end up writing a lot of overloaded methods and method chaining because we want to perform something extra with different values.

For example, if I say we need to call an API where I want to retrieve either 200 records or whatever value the user has passed. So this you can only achieve by writing two function calls.

But Kotlin has a feature where if no parameter is passed Kotlin picks up the default value if specified, thus overloaded methods can be drastically reduced. The following is the code where you can see how we used default parameters and it's one of the common use cases that is faced by every developer:

```
@GET("/1.1/statuses/home_timeline.json")
fun showHomeTimeline(@Query("count") count: Int = 200):
Call<List<Tweet>>
```

If you see and try to understand the preceding code, the function is expecting a count parameter, and count: Int = 200 says that if the parameter is not passed, the value of the count will be 200 and if the value is passed, then 200 will be replaced with a new given value.

Now, the previous function call is easily called in two ways:

- `timelineService.showHomeTimeline()` // This will return 200 records
- `timelineService.showHomeTimeline(500)` // If user wants more record user will pass desired value

Named parameter

We simply love this feature. A named parameter is something where you can bind the values with the parameter name, irrespective of the sequence of the parameter. The problem statement here is often that while dealing with the bad/legacy code, we came across two such methods where we have a huge list of parameters and we don't know which one is what parameter.

Assume that code is written like this:

```
fun complexMathCalculation(height: Int, scaleFactor: Float,
  displayValue: String, fromUser: Boolean, width: Int, colorCode:
  String): Int {
  // Code goes here
  return 0
  }
```

And somewhere it's getting called as follows:

```
fun void draw() {
    complexMathCalculation(10,5f,"Kotlin",true,50,"#FFFFFF");
  }
```

By looking at the preceding code we wonder if one can easily understand what those values are!

But if you try to call a function from Kotlin and use the concept of named parameter your code will look like the following:

```
complexMathCalculation(height = 10, scaleFactor = 5f, displayValue
  = "Kotlin", fromUser = true, width = 50, colorCode = "#FFFFFF")
```

Observe the parameter names before passing each of the values. Kotlin will bind those values to respected function parameters.

Someone will wonder why height and width parameters are not kept in sequence. We told you it's a bad/legacy code. Now, the crazy part is you being a good developer can call the same function as follows:

```
complexMathCalculation(height = 10, width = 50, scaleFactor = 5f,
    displayValue = "Kotlin", fromUser = true, colorCode = "#FFFFFF")
```

Observe the sequence of height and width parameters. Kotlin will bind the parameter in the correct way.

We have used this in the `StringExtension.kt` file. Take a look at the line where we are passing the `fromDate` and `toDate` parameters and referencing them with their names:

```
val (elapsedDays, elapsedHours, elapsedMinutes, elapsedSeconds) =
    getTimeDifference(fromDate = date, toDate = today)
```

 This feature only works when the function is written in Kotlin only. If you try to do the same for functions written in Java, you will have the warning **Named arguments are not allowed for non-Kotlin functions**.

Destructing declaration

Kotlin is loaded with features. Some of the features are beyond our imagination. What if we tell you a function can return multiple values! Or you can catch the objects into multiple variables. Destructing declaration allows you to perform such things.

Let's say we need to return two things from a function. For example, a result object and a status of some sort. A compact way of doing this in Kotlin is to declare a `data` class (`https://kotlinlang.org/docs/reference/data-classes.html`) and return its instance.

In Kotlin, we can achieve this by writing the following code:

```
data class Result(val result: Int, val status: Status)
fun function(...): Result {
  // computations

  return Result(result, status)
}

// Now, to use this function:
val (result, status) = function(...)
```

Observe how we break the `Result` object returned from the function and catch it inside two objects named `result` and `status`. You can use this object within its scope just like any other normal object. Isn't that interesting!

Basically, the preceding destructing declaration gets converted into the following type of code:

```
val result = result.result
val status = result.status
```

Take a look at `ProfileActivity`. We highlighted the destructing declaration as bold in the given code snippet:

```
apiHelper.getRequest(this, url, object : ApiListener {
  override fun onApiSuccess(apiResponse: ApiResponse) {
    val (id, firstName, lastName, headline,
    siteStandardProfileRequest) =
    Gson().fromJson(apiResponse.responseDataAsJson.toString(),
    LinkedInUser::class.java)
    txtUserName.text = "$firstName $lastName"
    txtHeadline.text = headline
  }

  override fun onApiError(liApiError: LIApiError) {
    toast("Can not retrieve your linked in profile")
  }
})
```

Another place where we have used the destructing declaration is our `StringExtension.kt` file. Where we want the `date` object to get destructed into pieces such as days, hours, minutes, and seconds:

```
val (elapsedDays, elapsedHours, elapsedMinutes, elapsedSeconds) =
getTimeDifference(fromDate = date, toDate = today)
```

The best place to use a destructing declaration can be iterating over the map:

```
for ((key, value) in map) {
  // do something with the key and the value
}
```

Android context

We all know how much of a key role context plays in Android. All Android components have context and they are capable of doing different things. Every time you need to access activity's context to pass it while displaying toast, dialogs, creating intent, and so on, we used to use `SomeActivity.this`. Kotlin will not allow this, but we have a slightly different way of doing this. We wanted to create `TweetView` and it was expecting context as a parameter. We can simply pass context like such this, observe `this@TweetDetailActivity`, which is nothing but `TweetDetailActivity.this`:

```
llTweets.addView(TweetView(this@TweetDetailActivity, result.data))
```

Null-Safety

Kotlin's most attractive feature and Java's *Billion Dollar mistake* is dealing with `NullPointerException`. Java code loves throwing `NullPointerException`. This always leads to a crash. We cannot afford a crash on production for such issues. There are ways of dealing with this. But what if we tell you that you can simply avoid it. We mean it! And if you use this feature properly your app will have less crashes in production.

Kotlin language automatically takes care of null handling. In the app, you will never notice null checks. We hardly need to worry about it.

Why Kotlin is called null-safe

In Java, the following code will throw `NullPointerException`, but it will still perfectly compile. Hence it never comes to our attention that we are coding an issue that can crash the application:

```
private Button createTweet=null;
createTweet.setOnClickListener(new View.OnClickListener() {
  @Override
  public void onClick(View view) {

  }
});
```

And the following code in Kotlin will give a compile-time error:

```
var createTweet: Button? = null
createTweet.setOnClickListener({
  // Do button click operation
})
```

That means Kotlin compiler is intelligent enough that it knows that `createTweet` can be null and until a developer does null checks code should not compile. Seems like it believes the *Prevention is better than cure* principle. Now let's try to handle the null check:

```
var num: Int? = null

if (num != null) {
  num.toString()
}
```

What will happen when we handle null checks like this, inside the `if` block `Int?` becomes `Int`. Inside the `if` block Kotlin is always aware of context and will never force us to do null checks. But this is not what Kotlin is made for!

Safe call operator (?.)

Kotlin has a syntax that replaces null checks. This is called the safe call or safe call operator:

```
num?.toFloat()
```

The preceding line returns the float conversion of the number if it is not null and null otherwise. While dealing with complex objects often we have chain calls that result in a lot of nested if. For example, the following nested if blocks:

```
if(linkedInUser!=null) {
  if (linkedInUser.siteStandardProfileRequest != null) {
    if (imageView != null) {
      imageView.show(linkedInUser.siteStandardProfileRequest.url);
    }
  }
}
```

This can be converted into one line, which is:

```
imageView?.show(linkedInUser?.siteStandardProfileRequest?.url)
```

Elvis operator (?:)

Many times we simply write an `if` condition to handle null check and return some static value if it is null. Kotlin has a solution to this stereotype code as well. It has an Elvis operator. An Elvis operator returns the alternate value if the object is found to be null:

```
var fileName:String?=null

val file= File(fileName?:"untitled.txt")
```

The preceding code will create a file with the name `untitled.txt` if the `fileName` string object is found null at the time of creating the file.

Force unwrap (!!)

However, often we know that an object is not null at the time of access, but since the type is nullable we have to do the null handling. In such situations, we have a way to insist that a compiler gives whatever value it has with the `!!` operator:

```
var num: Int? = null

num!!.div(10)
```

The preceding code will compile, but since we have used `!!`, the app will crash.

 While using !! make sure we are conscious. If we use just it to avoid compiler errors, we may need to deal with a lot of crashes. Use it in this very specific situation.

Smart casts

For type checks and casting, Kotlin provides two operators, `is` and `as`.

The is and !is operators

To check types we use `is` as an operator. It is similar to the `instanceof` operator in Java. But this type check is way smarter than Java.

The following Java code forces us to do type casting even if we have a condition for an `instanceof` check:

```
View view;

if(view instanceof Button){
    ((Button) view).setText("Some text");
}
```

Why double the work? Take a look at the Kotlin `is` operator. It automatically resolves all button functions for the `view` object. Now that's called a smart language:

```
val view: View
if (view is Button) {
  view.text = "Some text"
}
```

The as operator

The preceding automatic casting is known as smart cast. The `as` cast operator casts whatever value it's holding in the object into a given class type:

```
val tabLayout = findViewById(R.id.tabs) as TabLayout
```

The previous line will cast a view that has ID tabs into `TabLayout`. This is known as unsafe. Because what if tabs is the ID of some button or `TextView`. This instruction will fail and throw an exception. A better way to use it is, with the `safe` cast operator. So let's modify the instructions a bit. With safe cast operator it will look like the following:

```
val tabLayout = findViewById(R.id.tabs) as? TabLayout
tabLayout?.setupWithViewPager(container)
```

The `as?` will return null if the view is not of type `TabLayout`. And Kotlin handles null implicitly. So nothing to worry about now. The smart cast is also not required to cast it every time; once cast the `tabLayout` object can resolve all `TabLayout` class properties and functions.

Companion object

`Companion` is a keyword used in Kotlin. An object declaration inside a class can be marked as a `companion` object. All members of the `companion` object can be called using the class name directly. Sounds like static!

```
class MyClass {
  companion object Factory {
    fun create(): MyClass = MyClass()
  }
}
```

Calling can look as follows:

```
val instance = MyClass.create()
```

The name of a `companion` object can be omitted. There can be multiple `companion` objects inside a single class and they should have a name in this case.

Fragment instantiation using companion objects

We have to use a `companion` object to instantiate a fragment. Remember we have to use the `newInstance()` method to initialize a fragment because we cannot use the parameterized constructor for fragments. Our `UserTimeLineFragment` and `HomeTimeLineFragment` uses a `companion` object to help the fragment instantiation:

```
class UserTimeLineFragment : TwitterFragment() {
  override fun loadTimeline() {
    // Code goes here
  }

  companion object {

    /**
     * Use this factory method to create a new instance of
     * this fragment using the provided parameters.
     *
     * @return A new instance of fragment TwitterFragment.
     */
    fun newInstance(): UserTimeLineFragment =
      UserTimeLineFragment()
  }
}
```

Dealing with constants

Constants objects or variables are something where the value never changes throughout the life of an application. Do not make a mistake considering any `val` as constants. `val` are not constants, but they are immutable objects where a value once assigned cannot be changed, more like final objects in Java.

`Companion` objects do define constants that can be accessed in a static way. But the best way to define constants in Android is using a top-level file and dumping all your constants there.

To come to the conclusion of the previous line we did various experiments.

We started by using a simple `companion` object:

```
class Constants {
  companion object {
    val TWITTER_SUCCESS = 140
  }
}
```

Decompiling the preceding code results in the following:

```
public final class Constants {
  @NotNull
  private static final int TWITTER_SUCCESS = 140;
  public static final Constants.Companion Companion = new
   Constants.Companion((DefaultConstructorMarker)null);

  public static final class Companion {
    @NotNull
    public final String getTwitterSuccess() {
      return Constants.FOO;
    }

    private Companion() {
    }

    // synthetic method
    public Companion(DefaultConstructorMarker $constructor_marker)
     {
        this();
    }
  }
}
```

If you can make sense out of the preceding code it will have a call like:

```
Constants.Companion.getTwitterSuccess()
```

So, this introduces the static object and method, which is bad. Never use it. We can improve code by using the following two approaches:

```
class Constants {
  companion object {
    const val TWITTER_SUCCESS = 140
  }
}
```

The disadvantage is the getter is gone, and we actually have direct static access to the field now, but we still have a useless companion object generated by the compiler:

```
class Constants {
  companion object {
    @JvmField val TWITTER_SUCCESS = TWITTER_SUCCESS()
  }
}
```

There won't be any call to constants. `TWITTER_SUCCESS` in the second example, because the value is inlined.

After thinking more we decided to drop both the `companion` object and class, and simply have them as top-level file elements:

```
const val IS_CONNECTED_TO_SOCIAL_MEDIA =
 "is_connected_to_social_media"
const val IS_CONNECTED_TO_TWITTER = "is_connected_to_twitter"
const val IS_CONNECTED_TO_LINKEDIN = "is_connected_to_linkedin"

const val LINKEDIN_SUCCESS = 3672
const val TWITTER_SUCCESS = 140

const val TWEET_ID = "tweet_id"
```

Decompiling the preceding code surprisingly ends in perfect Java constant conversion:

```
public final class Constants {
  @NotNull
    public static final String TWITTER_SUCCESS = 140;
}
```

Great stuff!

 To see Kotlin's bytecode, Android Studio has an inbuilt option. In the menu go to **Tools** | **Kotlin** | **Show Kotlin bytecode**. You can see how Kotlin is making these magical things happen.

You can use these constants anywhere, anytime in the app without any headache of any import statements. Kotlin does it for you! Some of the places where we have used it are:

```
private var isConnectedToAnySocialMedia: Boolean by
  DelegatedPreference(this, IS_CONNECTED_TO_SOCIAL_MEDIA, false)

private var isConnectedToTwitter: Boolean by
  DelegatedPreference(this, IS_CONNECTED_TO_TWITTER, false)
```

```
private var isConnectedToLinkedIn: Boolean by
 DelegatedPreference(this, IS_CONNECTED_TO_LINKEDIN, false)
```

and

```
startActivity<TweetDetailActivity>(TWEET_ID to it.id)
```

 Never use `companion` objects to define constants. A separate constant file is always advisable to have. If you still want constant in the same file at least use `const val` together to achieve best possible optimization.

Object expressions and declarations

Sometimes we need to create an object with a slight modification of some class, without explicitly declaring a new subclass for it. Java handles this case with anonymous inner classes. Kotlin slightly generalizes this concept with object expressions and object declarations. Take a look at the following class:

```
timelineService.showHomeTimeline().enqueue(object :
 Callback<List<Tweet>>() {
   override fun success(result: Result<List<Tweet>>) {
     rvTimeline.layoutManager = LinearLayoutManager(context)
     rvTimeline.adapter = TweetAdapter(result.data) {
       startActivity<TweetDetailActivity>(TWEET_ID to it.id)
     }
   }

   override fun failure(exception: TwitterException) {
     toast(exception.message.toString())
   }
})
```

The `object` keyword can also be used to create objects of an anonymous class known as anonymous objects. We used this in `ProfileActivity.kt` as well. Take a look:

```
LISessionManager.getInstance(applicationContext)
 .init(this, buildScope(), object : AuthListener {
   override fun onAuthSuccess() {
     isConnectedToAnySocialMedia = true
     isConnectedToLinkedIn = true
     checkLinkedInIsConnected()
     toast("Connected to linked in, Token is ${LISessionManager
       .getInstance(applicationContext)
       .session.accessToken}")
```

```
    }

    override fun onAuthError(error: LIAuthError) {
        toast("Error connecting to linked in $error")
    }
}, true)
```

For an object as an expression, you can refer to the following example. There is an `Animal` class that has two functions. And we can catch its result in some object and that object can override all `open` functions:

```
open class Animal() {
    fun eat() = println("Eating...")

    open fun speak() = println("Making different sound...")
}
```

The caller function can have code like the following:

```
val dog = object : Animal() {
    override fun speak() = println("This is dog and it's barking...")
}

dog.eat()
dog.speak()
```

We override the `talk` method and `dog.talk()` will print **This is dog and it's barking**....

Delegated properties

If you try to break down the words you will see two words, delegate, and property. The name itself says that you delegate something in the form of property. Basically corresponding `getValue()` and `setValue()` methods will be called when you try to access any of the variables. They are not backed by class fields, but it delegates works to some other piece of code.

In the following list, we will start to explain a few terms:

- `lazy{}`: This is a built-in delegated property method. It will execute lines within the lazy block when a variable, that is, prefs is referenced first.

- `getValue()`: This is responsible for to passing the current state or value of the variable when it is read (when it's on the right side of the = operator). The following is the code and explanation about the parameter of `getValue()`:

```
operator fun getValue(thisRef: Any?, property: KProperty<*>): T
{
  return findPreferences(key, defaultValue)
}
```

- `thisRef`: This is a reference to the class that the property is in.
- `property`: This is a reflection description of the property being delegated.

Unlike `getValue()`, `setValue()` is used to set the updated value of the property when it is being written (when it's on the left side of an = operator). The following is the code and explanation about the parameter of `setValue()`:

```
operator fun setValue(thisRef: Any?, property: KProperty<*>, value:
 T) {
   savePreference(key, value)
}
```

- `thisRef`: This is a reference to the class that the property is in
- `property`: This is a reflection description of the property being delegated
- `value`: This is the new value of the property

Dealing with Shared Preferences

Shared Preferences in Android is very much crucial. It's a great persistent storage type. It's very easy to use, but not simple. We all know the pain we have to take while initializing them, but also while saving data into it we need to take care of the editor's object, and above all, we cannot forget about the apply method to use. This is popularly known as ceremonies of API. We have to call multiple methods every time to get any task done.

Now, while opening the app we want to check whether the user has connected to any of the accounts. We can read the value from the `SharedPreferences` with the following mentioned single line code:

```
private var isConnectedToAnySocialMedia: Boolean by
  PreferenceExtension(this, IS_CONNECTED_TO_SOCIAL_MEDIA, false)
```

Let's see how this entire thing can be done:

```
class PreferenceExtension<T>(val context: Context, val key: String,
 val defaultValue: T) {
  val prefs: SharedPreferences by lazy {
    context.getSharedPreferences(context.getString
     (R.string.app_name), Context.MODE_PRIVATE) }

  operator fun getValue(thisRef: Any?, property: KProperty<*>): T {
    return findPreferences(key, defaultValue)
  }

  operator fun setValue(thisRef: Any?,
  property: KProperty<*>, value: T) {
    savePreference(key, value)
  }

  @Suppress("UNCHECKED_CAST")
  private fun findPreferences(key: String, defaultValue: T): T {
    with(prefs)
    {
        val result: Any = when (defaultValue) {
            is Boolean -> getBoolean(key, defaultValue)
            is Int -> getInt(key, defaultValue)
            is Long -> getLong(key, defaultValue)
            is Float -> getFloat(key, defaultValue)
            is String -> getString(key, defaultValue)
            else -> throw IllegalArgumentException()
        }
        return result as T
    }
}

  @SuppressLint("CommitPrefEdits")
  private fun savePreference(key: String, value: T) {
    with(prefs.edit())
    {
        when (value) {
            is Boolean -> putBoolean(key, value)
            is Int -> putInt(key, value)
            is Long -> putLong(key, value)
            is Float -> putFloat(key, value)
            is String -> putString(key, value)
            else -> throw IllegalArgumentException()
        }.apply()
    }
  }
}
```

Have a look at the class again, and relate them to an explanation of the `lazy {}`, `getValue()`, and `setValue()` methods.

Setting up an item click on RecyclerView

`RecyclerView` is also a very core part of Android application development. You won't find an app that is not using `RecyclerView`. We love it, but we also miss `setOnItemClickListener()` of `ListView` don't we? Well, what if we tell you that instead of having a listener every time for it we can simply define what to do using Lambdas. With Kotlin it's possible.

To understand this properly we need to go a bit deeper into functions and operators. Kotlin has various operators overloaded such as unary operators, binary operators, indexed access operator, invoke operator, equality and inequality operator, and augmented assignments. The `invoke()` operator will help us easily write an item listener. Let's try to understand it a bit:

Expression	Translated to
a()	a.invoke()
a(i)	a.invoke(i)
a(i, j)	a.invoke(i, j)
a(i_1, ..., i_n)	a.invoke(i_1, ..., i_n)

Parentheses are translated to calls to invoke with an appropriate number of arguments.

Using the same concept we can have an interface like the following:

```
interface OnRecyclerViewItemClickListener {
  operator fun invoke(tweet: Tweet)
}
```

And when needed we can call it as follows:

```
itemView(tweet)
```

Which is as good as:

```
itemView.invoke(tweet)
```

Our view holder is already responsible for binding the data in the showData function:

```
class ViewHolder(val view: View, val callback: (Tweet) -> Unit) :
 RecyclerView.ViewHolder(view) {
  private var imgProfilePic: ImageView
  private var txtName: TextView
  private var txtHandler: TextView
  private var txtTweet: TextView
  private var imgMedia: ImageView
  private var txtTweetTime: TextView

  init {
    imgProfilePic = itemView.findViewById(R.id.imgProfilePic)
    txtName = itemView.findViewById(R.id.txtName)
    txtHandler = itemView.findViewById(R.id.txtHandler)
    txtTweet = itemView.findViewById(R.id.txtTweet)
    imgMedia = itemView.findViewById(R.id.imgMedia)
    txtTweetTime = itemView.findViewById(R.id.txtTweetTime)
  }

  fun showData(tweet: Tweet) {
    with(tweet) {
      imgProfilePic.setRoundedImageOption
       (user.profileImageUrlHttps)
      txtName.text = user.name
      txtHandler.text = "@${user.screenName}"
      txtTweet.text = text
      //Working on this right now getting some exception
       txtTweetTime.text = createdAt.getDateInHours()
      if (entities.media.isNotEmpty()) {
        imgMedia.visible()
        imgMedia.setImageLazy(entities.media[0].mediaUrlHttps)
      } else {
         imgMedia.gone()
         }
         itemView.setOnClickListener { callback(this) }
    }
  }
}
```

The `TweetAdapter` class will have an item click listener as a parameter of the constructor:

```kotlin
class TweetAdapter(val items: List<Tweet>, val callback: (Tweet) ->
Unit) : RecyclerView.Adapter<TweetAdapter.ViewHolder>() {

  override fun onCreateViewHolder(parent: ViewGroup, viewType:
   Int): ViewHolder {
    return
     ViewHolder(LayoutInflater.from(parent.context)
     .inflate(R.layout.tweet_list_item, parent, false),
     callback)
   }

  override fun getItemCount(): Int = items.size

  override fun onBindViewHolder(holder: ViewHolder, position: Int)
  {
    holder.showData(items[position])
  }

  class ViewHolder(val view: View, val callback: (Tweet) -> Unit) :
   RecyclerView.ViewHolder(view) {
    private var imgProfilePic: ImageView
    private var txtName: TextView
    private var txtHandler: TextView
    private var txtTweet: TextView
    private var imgMedia: ImageView
    private var txtTweetTime: TextView

    init {
      imgProfilePic = itemView.findViewById(R.id.imgProfilePic)
      txtName = itemView.findViewById(R.id.txtName)
      txtHandler = itemView.findViewById(R.id.txtHandler)
      txtTweet = itemView.findViewById(R.id.txtTweet)
      imgMedia = itemView.findViewById(R.id.imgMedia)
      txtTweetTime = itemView.findViewById(R.id.txtTweetTime)
    }

    fun showData(tweet: Tweet) {
      with(tweet) {
        imgProfilePic.setRoundedImageOption
         (user.profileImageUrlHttps)
        txtName.text = user.name
        txtHandler.text = "@${user.screenName}"
        txtTweet.text = text
        //Working on this right now getting some exception
        txtTweetTime.text = createdAt.getDateInHours()
        if (entities.media.isNotEmpty()) {
```

```
            imgMedia.visible()
            imgMedia.setImageLazy(entities.media[0].mediaUrlHttps)
        } else {
            imgMedia.gone()
          }
        itemView.setOnClickListener { callback(this) }
      }
    }
  }
}
```

And our `HomeTimeLineFragment` will consume an adapter like this:

```
rvTimeline.layoutManager = LinearLayoutManager(context)
rvTimeline.adapter = TweetAdapter(result.data) {
  startActivity<TweetDetailActivity>(TWEET_ID to it.id)
}
```

Now, to understand it thoroughly, we actually created an object that implements our interface. Which is far, far better than having an anonymous class.

Anko - Kotlin's buddy for Android

We can't tell you how much we love this library. It is that significant that in our Android chapter we are dedicating a few pages to it. Kotlin as a language can be used in multiple places, for example, Spring Boot, Android, JavaScript, and so on. While Anko is focusing on making Android app development easier and faster, it has all those optimizations, tricks, and magic that is missing in Kotlin.

Anko consists of several sets of APIs, originally mentioned at `https://github.com/Kotlin/anko`:

- **Anko commons**: This is a helper library full of APIs for intents, dialogs, logging, and so on
- **Anko layouts**: This is a cool new way to write dynamic Android layouts. It's fast and type-safe
- **Anko SQLite**: This is a package containing query **DSL** (**Domain Specific Language**) and parsers dealing with SQLite in Android projects
- **Anko coroutines**: The `kotlinx.coroutines` (`https://github.com/Kotlin/kotlinx.coroutines`) library and utilities

Setting up Anko

Anko has a Gradle-based project that can be plugged in by adding a single line inside app level `build.gradle`. This dependency will load all Anko features and functions into the app:

```
dependencies {
  compile fileTree(include: ['*.jar'], dir: 'libs')
  androidTestCompile('com.android.support.test.espresso:espresso-
  core:2.2.2', {
    exclude group: 'com.android.support', module: 'support-
    annotations'
  })
  compile "org.jetbrains.kotlin:kotlin-stdlib-jre7:$kotlin_version"
  compile "org.jetbrains.anko:anko:$anko_version"

  // Other libs and gradle dependencies

  testCompile 'junit:junit:4.12'
}
```

There are also a number of artifacts for the Android support libraries. Find more at `https:/ /github.com/Kotlin/anko`:

```
dependencies {
  // Appcompat-v7 (only Anko Commons)
  compile "org.jetbrains.anko:anko-appcompat-v7-
   commons:$anko_version"

  // Appcompat-v7 (Anko Layouts)
  compile "org.jetbrains.anko:anko-appcompat-v7:$anko_version"
  compile "org.jetbrains.anko:anko-coroutines:$anko_version"

  // CardView-v7
  compile "org.jetbrains.anko:anko-cardview-v7:$anko_version"

  // Design
  compile "org.jetbrains.anko:anko-design:$anko_version"
  compile "org.jetbrains.anko:anko-design-coroutines:$anko_version"

  // GridLayout-v7
  compile "org.jetbrains.anko:anko-gridlayout-v7:$anko_version"

  // Percent
  compile "org.jetbrains.anko:anko-percent:$anko_version"

  // RecyclerView-v7
  compile "org.jetbrains.anko:anko-recyclerview-v7:$anko_version"
```

```
    compile "org.jetbrains.anko:anko-recyclerview-v7-
      coroutines:$anko_version"

    // Support-v4 (only Anko Commons)
    compile "org.jetbrains.anko:anko-support-v4-
      commons:$anko_version"

    // Support-v4 (Anko Layouts)
    compile "org.jetbrains.anko:anko-support-v4:$anko_version"
}
```

Let's explore!

Displaying toast()

We love displaying toast! For displaying validation messages to the user, flashing an error message, and sometimes for debugging too.

And we know how many times we have missed using `.show()` methods. Every time we pass context setting up a duration. How about having a simple function that takes care of all of this. Yes! With Kotlin this is also true. Anko commons has functions displaying toast in an easy way.

With Anko you can display toast, for example:

```
import org.jetbrains.anko.toast

toast(exception.message.toString())
```

Starting an activity made easy

Tell me, how many times have you used the following code to start an `Activity`?

```
Intent intent = new Intent(CurrentActivity.this,
  NextActivity.class);
intent.putExtra("key", value); //Optional parameters
CurrentActivity.this.startActivity(intent);
```

Countless times, isn't it? And we know it's boring. But now with the help of Anko, we can start activity very easily. Anko's `Intents.kt` has a few extension functions using which we can start the activity. Take a look at the code in `AppToolbar.kt`, on clicking the menu we are starting `ProfileActivity`:

```
toolbar.context.startActivity<ProfileActivity>()
```

The code looks so much cleaner with no verbosity. But starting an activity is not always that simple. We also sometimes need some values as a part of extras. You can pass them as a part of variable arguments. We are starting the `TweetDetailActivity` with `TWEET_ID` as a parameter:

```
startActivity<TweetDetailActivity>(TWEET_ID to it.id)
```

Since the `startActivity` function can have variable arguments, multiple extras can be passed:

```
startActivity<SomeActivity>("id" to 5, "name" to "John")
```

Anko layout

Using DSL, Anko also supports creating dynamic layouts. Just to give you an idea, the following code can create a simple `EditText` with a `button` following it:

```
verticalLayout {
  val name = editText()
  button("Say Hello") {
    onClick { toast("Hello, ${name.text}!") }
  }
}
```

And the screen will look like the following:

Summary

If you are reading this summary, we hope you have read this entire chapter. You have learned to apply Kotlin in Android app development. The app covers many basic features and usages of language that almost any Android can contain.

The chapter is the crux of what we have learned so far while working on Kotlin. There can be many other usages and variations in the example and implementation you will find in the vast world of the internet and while discussing with the community.

The purpose of this chapter was to show how specific Android problems can be solved by applying Kotlin. We tried to cover as much as possible, giving full justice to language and platform.

And we have also learned a lot of things while writing this chapter. The app is written using Kotlin version 1.1.4. Kotlin will evolve very fast. We will keep you updated with future Kotlin versions.

In the next chapter, we will see Kotlin in action, how Kotlin gets compiled, and takes the form of JavaScript and runs on the browser. *There is more to come than meets the eye.*

4

Weather App Using Kotlin for JavaScript

In previous chapters, we saw Kotlin gelling together with Sprint Boot and Android very well. In the same way, Kotlin will give you a smooth experience while using it on the browser side as well. With JavaScript, initially, there was nothing but lightweight code running on a client side to validate user input, show tooltips, and so on. With all the latest frameworks, that is, Node.js, Angular.js, Express.js; JavaScript is no longer a child. They are very mature platforms on which big systems can rely. After Kotlin announced support for JavaScript, it was a wonderful moment for us. One can really be a full-stack developer, using Kotlin mobile apps, writing API, and creating beautiful web pages can be developed. Amazing! We feel it's the golden age of JavaScript. JavaScript has been playing a key role when it comes to web and browser. But the code writing is still boring. Kotlin makes writing JavaScript code a lot more fun and you will agree with us as you move through this chapter.

In this chapter, we will be covering JavaScript from a browser perspective. We will create a single page web app that will show the weather forecast for seven days from the current date. The user will provide a ZIP code as input for which the weather will be displayed. We will display all the basic information about the weather on a given day. We believe in learning by doing practicals. Let's see the power of Kotlin from a browser perspective.

Conceptually, we will cover the following points while making a web app:

- Setting up a project to use Kotlin along with JavaScript
- Showing simple text using Kotlin code
- Interacting with **Document Object Model** (**DOM**) using Kotlin
- DSL and usage of `kotlinx.html`
- Interoperability with JavaScript

Creating your first Kotlin and JavaScript project

Tighten your shoelaces! As a first step, we will do the setup and create a simple app that prints on a console and changes the background color of a page.

Choosing an IDE

From Microsoft Visual Studio, NetBeans to Eclipse and Code::Blocks, we have a series of great and powerful IDEs. Each of them has their own pros and cons. JetBrains is one of the giants that is famous for its cutting-edge software and IntelliJ IDEA Ultimate is considered among one of the most intelligent IDEs for Java. It supports Kotlin and JavaScript by default. There is no other hassle in setting up the environments. Just install it from `https://www.jetbrains.com/idea` and you are all set to create your first JavaScript project using Kotlin.

Creating a project

If you are all done with setting up an IDE, launch IntelliJ IDEA and select **Create New Project**. You will then have the following screen opened. Select **Kotlin | Kotlin (JavaScript)** options as shown in the following screenshot:

Make sure you select **Kotlin (JavaScript)** as highlighted in the preceding screenshot. The next step is to provide your **Project name** and choose a destination for your project directory:

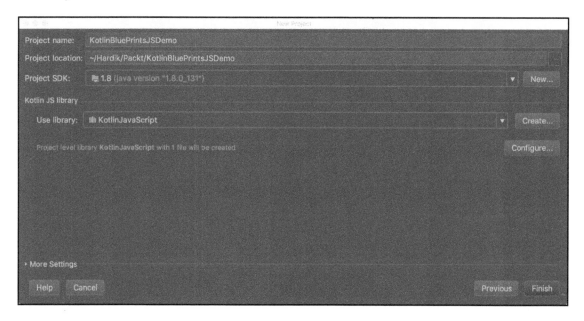

Creating an HTML page

No browser project is complete without an HTML page. Create an `index.html` page in the root directory of your project. And write the following lines in a `<body>` tag:

```html
<body>
  <script type="text/javascript"
    src="out/production/KotlinWeb/lib/kotlin.js"></script>
  <script type="text/javascript"
    src="out/production/KotlinWeb/KotlinWeb.js"></script>
</body>
```

Creating a Main.kt file

After creating our `index.html` page. Let's create our first Kotlin file. Name it as `Main.kt` or provide any desired name. Create a file in the `src` folder and write the following function inside:

```kotlin
fun main(args: Array<String>) {
  document.bgColor="FF0000"
  val message = "Kotlin Blueprints"
  println("Your first JS code using Kotlin")
}
```

Build the project, by selecting the **Build** | **Build Project menu** option. On expanding the project explorer on the left of your workspace you will have the following type of directory structure:

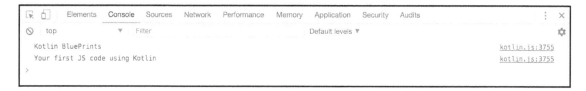

Make sure you double-check that the `<script>` tags are added in the `<body>`. They should match the name with the files created inside `out/production/KotlinBluePrintsJSDemo/`.

Running the project

If you have followed all the steps simply execute your `index.html` file in any browser and you should see the following output on your console and a red colored page rendered on your DOM:

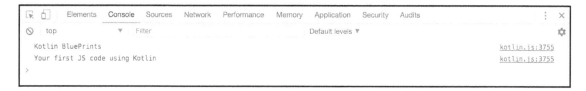

Congratulations! You have executed your first Kotlin code on the browser.

Since we have code written in Kotlin, source code needs to recompile every time we update the code. Simply reloading an HTML page will not work. So build your project from the **Build** | **Build Project** menu option.

Developing a weather forecast web app

It was fun writing Kotlin code for a browser and see it working, wasn't it? Now we should target bigger goals. Let's develop another app step by step. We will build a weather forecast app, where the user will enter a ZIP code and can see the weather details (seven day forecast) for the provided region. We will use the OpenWeatherMap API to get the weather details. Please find more details at `https://openweathermap.org/api`.

Before we move to the next step we should create a new project named `KotlinBluePrintsJSDemo`. Some quick steps to follow:

1. Create a Kotlin+JavaScript project named `KotlinBluePrintsJSDemo`.
2. Create an `index.html` page under the root directory.
3. Create a `Main.kt` file inside the `src` directory.
4. Add script tags to add two JavaScript files, `kotlin.js` and `KotlinBluePrintsJSDemo.js`.
5. Build a project.

We want to create an app that will look like this at the end. Entirely in Kotlin:

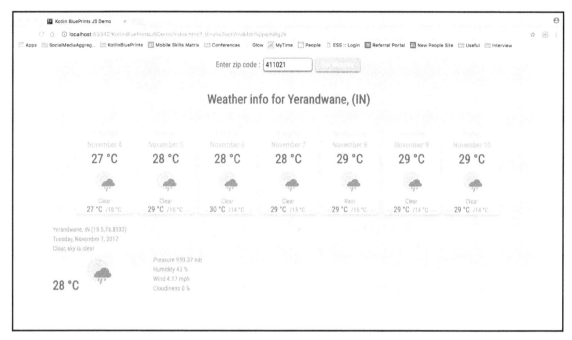

Creating a UI with dummy data

The very first thing we do is to create a dummy view and get a clear idea of how our HTML page will look. We will also use a bit of CSS to give basic styles to our <div> tags.

Simple HTML approach

Now we shall look at the index.html file that we created by writing the following code. It's boring plain HTML tags:

```
<!DOCTYPE html>
<html lang="en">
<head>
  <meta charset="UTF-8">
  <title>Kotlin BluePrints JS Demo</title>
</head>
<body>
  <link rel="stylesheet" type="text/css" href="css/main.css">
  <div id="container">
```

```html
      <label>Enter zip code : <input id="zipCode" type="number">
        </label>
      <button id="submitZipCode" type="button">Get Weather</button>

      <div class="weatherContainer">
        <div class="weatherBlock">
          <div>13 Oct, 2017</div>
            <img src="images/weather_img.png" height="40px"
              width="40px">
          <div> <span>35</span> <span>20</span> </div>
        </div>
        <div class="weatherBlock">
          <div>13 Oct, 2017</div>
            <img src="images/weather_img.png" height="40px"
              width="40px">
            <div> <span>35</span> <span>20</span> </div>
          </div>
          <!-- Similarly you can have remaining divs here -->
          </div>
        </div>

<script src="out/production/KotlinBluePrintsJSDemo/lib/kotlin.js">
  </script>
<script
  src="out/production/KotlinBluePrintsJSDemo
  /KotlinBluePrintsJSDemo.js"></script>

</body>
</html>
```

Observe two tags, `<script>` and `<link>`. We haven't added CSS yet. Let's create a CSS folder under the root directory and create a `main.css` file inside. The `main.css` will contain the following code for now:

```css
.weatherContainer {
  width: 90%;
  background: #EEEEEE;
  margin: 10px auto;
  position: relative;
  text-align:center;
}

.weatherBlock {
  background: #FFFFFF;
  height: 100px;
  width: 100px;
  display:inline-block;
  margin: 10px;
```

```
    }
```

In a source code, we have also created an `images` directory and put some weather images in it to make the UI more beautiful.

Creating UI using Kotlin

The `index.html` page contains all the HTML code. We need to now move that HTML code to Kotlin. Kotlin has the capability to manipulate the DOM element and it can also deal with the tree elements and their hierarchy.

Simply put two `<script>` tags and a parent `<div>` tag in an HTML page and everything will go to a Kotlin page:

```
<div id="container">

</div>
```

Now, in `Main.kt` we will write the HTML code that we previously wrote inside `index.html`. `Main.kt` and it will look as follows:

```
fun main(args: Array<String>) {
  createUserInput()
}

fun createUserInput() {
  val root = document.getElementById("container")
  root?.innerHTML = "<label>Enter zip code : <input id=\"zipCode\"
   type=\"number\"></label>" +
        "<button id=\"submitZipCode\" type=\"button\">Get
        Weather</button>" +
        "<div class=\"weatherContainer\">" +
        "<div class=\"weatherBlock\">" +
        "<div>13 Oct, 2017</div>" +
        "<img src=\"images/weather_img.png\" height=\"40px\"
         width=\"40px\">"+
        "<div>" +
        "<span>35</span>" +
        "<span>20</span>" +
        "</div>" +
        "</div>" +
        "<div class=\"weatherBlock\">" +
        "<div>13 Oct, 2017</div>" +
        "<img src=\"images/weather_img.png\" height=\"40px\"
         width=\"40px\">"+
        "<div>" +
```

```
            "<span>35</span>" +
            "<span>20</span>" +
            "</div>" +
            "</div>"
        // Similarly add remaining divs
    }
```

Take a note of the `document` object and its function `getElementById`. This is coming from the `kotlin.browser.document` package. Also `org.w3c.dom` as `companion` classes for all HTML elements.

With object root, we get access to an `innerHTML` property and we can assign any valid HTML strings to it and it will get rendered.

It is noteworthy that the nullability of root objects is handled with Null Safety operator `?` of Kotlin.

What is DSL?

Now, the previous approach doesn't create much difference. Kotlin would want to do better! Let us introduce you to the beautiful concept of DSL. **DSL** stands for **Domain Specific Language**. As the name indicates, it gives you the feeling that you are writing code in a language, using terminology particular to a given domain, without being geeky, but then this terminology is cleverly embedded as a syntax in a powerful language. If you are from the Groovy community you must be aware of builders. Groovy builders allow defining data in a semi declarative way. It's a kind of mini-language of its own. Builders are considered good for generating XML and laying out UI components. Kotlin DSL uses Lambdas a lot.

 DSL in Kotlin are type-safe builders. It means we can detect compilation errors in IntelliJ's beautiful IDE. The type-check builders are much better than the dynamically-typed builders of Groovy.

Using Kotlinx.html

The DSL to build HTML trees is a pluggable dependency. We, therefore, need to set it up and configure it for our project. For now, we will keep things simple and add the dependency in them in the form of a `.jar` file. We will keep this `.jar` file in the `lib` folder, which will reside at the root level.

The library is created by the JetBrains team only and it's open source. You can find it at `https://github.com/Kotlin/kotlinx.html`. You can simply visit the URL `https://dl.bintray.com/kotlin/kotlinx.html/org/jetbrains/kotlinx/kotlinx-html-js/0.6.4/` and download the `.jar` file from there. For this demo app, we have used v 0.6.4.

The `.jar` repository page can look as follows:

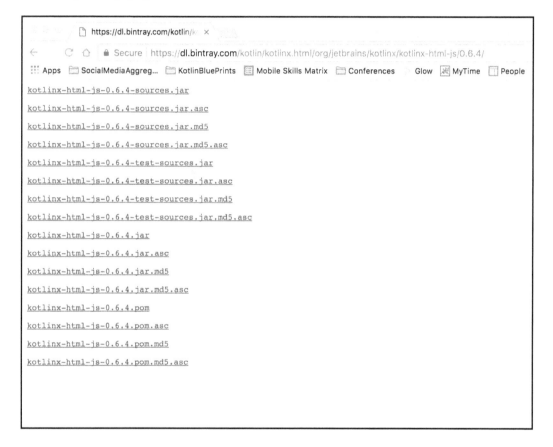

To set up the `kotlinx.html` dependency in your app please follow these steps:

1. In our app, we are using v 0.6.4. Make sure you download the JAR file named `kotlinx-html-js-0.6.4.jar`.
2. Please verify that you have kept the `.jar` file inside the `lib` directory.
3. Also, do not forget to add the `.jar` file as a library.
4. Right-click on the `.jar` file and select `Add As Library....`

5. Select classes as a category while adding them as a library. Or you can simply choose to add the dependency via Gradle, in that, you need to add the following things to your `build.gradle` file:

```
repositories {
  jcenter()
}
dependencies {
  //Fill this in with the version of kotlinx in use in your
  project
  def kotlinx_html_version = "your_version_here"
  // include for client-side
  compile "org.jetbrains.kotlinx:kotlinx-html-
  js:${kotlinx_html_version}"
}
```

Refactoring the HTML code using DSL

The DSL code to make a button with the title "`Get Weather`" looks as follows:

```
button {
  +"Get Weather"
  type = ButtonType.button
  onClickFunction = {
    // Your code to handle button click goes here.
  }
}
```

Simple and clean code.

Similarly, let's create a function that will display an entire `div`, which has a `label`, text input, and `button`:

```
fun getInputDiv(): HTMLDivElement {
  val inputDiv = document.create.div {
    label {
      +"Enter zip code : "
      input {
        id = "zipCode"
        type = InputType.number
        value = 411021.toString()
      }
    }
    button {
      +"Get Weather"
      type = ButtonType.button
```

```
        onClickFunction = {
          // Your code to handle button click goes here
        }
      }
    }
    return inputDiv
  }
```

Observe how we have provided ID, input types, and a default ZIP code value. A default ZIP code value is optional.

Let's spend some time understanding the previous code. `label`, `input`, `button`, `type`, `id`, and `onClickFunction` are nothing but functions. They are basically Lambda functions.

Some of the functions that use Lambda parameters and call variations can be as follows:

```
someFunction({})
```

```
someFunction("KotlinBluePrints",1,{})
```

```
someFunction("KotlinBluePrints",1){}
```

```
someFunction{}
```

Let's run the code. You may get an error on the console saying:

```
Error Uncaught Error: Error loading module 'KotlinBluePrintsJSDemo'. Its
dependency 'kotlinx-html-js' was not found. Please, check whether 'kotlinx-
html-js' is loaded prior to 'KotlinBluePrintsJSDemo'.
```

This is because `kotlinx-html-js` is missing, which is required to process the DSL generated code. You can see the `kotlinx-html-js` file generated under the `out/production/KotlinBluePrintsJSDemo/lib` path.

Calling a weather API

Now it's time to get the weather data and display it on the page.

We will use `XMLHttpRequest` to achieve this. Register yourself at `http://openweathermap.org/appid` and get your application ID. Your application ID will be appended in the actual URL to make the authenticated call to the weather API. Once you get the app ID let's keep that information in the `Constants.kt` file:

```
const val IMAGE_URL = "http://openweathermap.org/img/w/%s.png"
```

```
const val BASE_URL =
```

```
        "https://api.openweathermap.org/data/2.5/forecast/daily?
          mode=json&units=metric&cnt=7"
        const val APP_ID = "Your open weather map application id"
        const val FULL_URL = "$BASE_URL&appid=$APP_ID&q="
```

The `Constants.kt` file is not as simple as it looks. Check how we have stored different values. We have used `const val`, which is equivalent to `const` and static used combined. Also defining `FULL_URL` uses the concept of string interpolation. String interpolation is used to concatenate static strings along with string objects. You can also call functions in string interpolation as follows:

```
        h4 {
          +"Weather info for ${forecastResult.city.name},
            (${forecastResult.city.country})"
        }
```

Now, in `onClickFunction` we write the following code to perform the API call and on the successful response we call a `showData` function, which takes a `forecastResult` object:

```
        onClickFunction = {
          val zipCode = document.getElementById("zipCode") as
            HTMLInputElement
          val xmlHttpRequest = XMLHttpRequest()
          xmlHttpRequest.open("GET", FULL_URL + zipCode.value, false)
          xmlHttpRequest.send()
          println(xmlHttpRequest.responseText)
          val forecastResult = JSON.parse<ForecastResult>
          (xmlHttpRequest.responseText)
          showData(forecastResult)
        }
```

Reading data from input elements

See how we read data from input elements:

```
        document.getElementById("zipCode") as HTMLInputElement
```

The `as HTMLInputElement` construct is basically casting a result into the `HTMLInputElement` class.

Using `as` directly is not advisable because it can give you `ClassCastException`; a proper way to use it is `as?` `HTMLInputElement`. This returns null if the class cast fails. And Kotlin will force you to use a Null Safety operator from that very moment.

Data classes

We are maintaining `ForecastResult`, which is our model. For this purpose, we have data classes in Kotlin. One of the coolest features in Kotlin is data classes. All the pain that we used to endure to create and maintain POJO classes in Java is gone. No need to have those dedicated packages to hold your model class. Any Kotlin file can hold your `data` class. By default it provides you methods such as `toString()`, `equals()`, `copy()`, and `hashCode()` method implementation. In Android, we mostly use these types of classes to hold our JSON responses in the form of model classes. You can check out the data classes we created in `ServerResponses.kt`:

```
data class ForecastResult(val city: City, val list:
 Array<Forecast>)

data class City(val id: Long, val name: String, val coord:
 Coordinates, val country: String, val population: Int)

data class Coordinates(val lon: Float, val lat: Float)

data class Forecast(val dt: Long, val temp: Temperature, val
 pressure: Float, val humidity: Int, val weather: Array<Weather>,
 val speed: Float, val deg: Int, val clouds: Int)

data class Temperature(val day: Float, val min: Float, val max:
 Float, val night: Float, val eve: Float, val morn: Float)

data class Weather(val id: Long, val main: String, val description:
 String, val icon: String)
```

Some of the points to consider while using data classes are:

- The primary constructor needs to have at least one parameter
- All primary constructor parameters need to be marked as `val` or `var`
- Data classes cannot be abstract, open, sealed, or inner
- (Before version 1.1) data classes may only implement interfaces

Showing data to the user

Now comes the interesting part. We gate a `ForecastResult` object, which holds all the records. The `list` object holds records for seven days. Let's create a `showData` function that takes a `ForecastResult` object and display title text in <h4>. The code will look like the following snippet. Also, it has yet again one more example of string interpolation:

```kotlin
fun showData(forecastResult: ForecastResult) {
    val root = document.getElementById("container")
    root?.appendChild(document.create.div(classes = "currentTemp") {
        h4 {
            +"Weather info for ${forecastResult.city.name}
             (${forecastResult.city.country})"
        }
    })
}
```

This is simple now, quickly create a `showForecast` function that will be called from `showData` and will display the weather forecast for seven days. The `showForecast` is used with a function from Kotlin. `thewith()` is one of those functions that is liked by the developer community a lot; it makes use of Kotlin sweeter. The `with()` function accepts the receiver and the code written inside the function automatically applies to the receiver object. It's an inline function. Check out the following document:

```kotlin
/** * Calls the specified function [block] with the given [receiver] as its
receiver and returns its result. */
public inline fun <T, R> with(receiver: T, block: T.() -> R): R =
receiver.block()
```

In the code, observe how each iteration is using a `with` block. We have removed some of the lines from the original code, so that we can have the clean code snippet here:

```kotlin
forecastResult.list.forEachIndexed { index, forecast ->
    with(forecast)
    {
        weatherContainer.appendChild(document.create.div(classes =
          "weatherBlock") {
            div {
                p(classes = "currentTemp") {
                    +"${Math.round(temp.day)} °C"
                }
            }
            img(classes = "weatherImage") {
              src = "images/weather_img.png"
            }
            div {
```

```
        span(classes = "secondaryText") {
          +weather[0].main
        }
      }
      div {
        with(temp) {
          span(classes = "primaryText") { +"${Math.round(max)}
            °C"
        }
        span(classes = "secondaryText") { +"
         /${Math.round(min)} °C" }
        }
      }
      onClickFunction = {
        showDetailedForecast(forecastResult.city, forecast)
      }
    })
  }
}
```

DSL and Kotlin code is now beautifully gelled. Also notice the `onClickFunction` that we wrote on `div`. Sweet, isn't it?

Showing weather details

A very small part of the app is left now. Let's show some more details to the user. Along with this, we will also learn a few more features of Kotlin. We have created a `showDetailedForecast` function that takes the `City` and `Forecast` objects as parameters. The following code snippets provide two things to learn:

```
fun showDetailedForecast(city: City, forecast: Forecast) {
  val root = document.getElementById("container")
  val weatherDetailDiv = document.create.div(classes =
    "detailsContainer")
  val basicDetailDiv = document.create.div {
    p(classes = "secondaryText") {
      +"${city.name}, ${city.country}
        (${city.coord.lat},${city.coord.lon})"
    }
    p(classes = "secondaryText") {
      +forecast.dt.getFullDate()
    }
    p(classes = "secondaryText") {
      +"${forecast.weather[0].main},
        ${forecast.weather[0].description}"
    }
```

```
    }
    val otherDetailsDiv = document.create.div {
      div {
        id = "leftDiv"
        span(classes = "currentTemp") {
          +"${Math.round(forecast.temp.day)} °C"
        }
        img {
          src = "images/weather_img.png"
          width = 90.toString()
          height = 90.toString()
        }
      }
      div {
        id = "rightDiv"
        p(classes = "secondaryText") { +"Pressure:
          ${forecast.pressure}
         mb" }
        p(classes = "secondaryText") { +"Humidity:
          ${forecast.humidity}
         %" }
        p(classes = "secondaryText") { +"Wind: ${forecast.speed} mph" }
        p(classes = "secondaryText") { +"Cloudiness:
          ${forecast.clouds}
         %" }

      }
      div(classes = "clearBoth")
    }

    weatherDetailDiv.appendChild(basicDetailDiv)
    weatherDetailDiv.appendChild(otherDetailsDiv)

    root?.appendChild(weatherDetailDiv)
    }
```

Named parameters

In Kotlin, we can call/bind a parameter with their name for any function. We can call the preceding function by interchanging the parameter sequence as well. Something like the following:

```
showDetailedForecast(forecast = forecast, city =
  forecastResult.city)
```

Observe that we swapped the place of the variable. And no wonder, all CSS classes that we have applied so far have a named parameter. Check all previous `<div>`, `<h>`, and `<p>` tags. Consider the following examples:

```
val weatherDetailDiv = document.create.div(classes =
  "detailsContainer")

button(classes = "getWeatherButton")

span(classes = "primaryText") { +"${Math.round(max)} °C" }
```

Extension functions

Extension functions are a beautiful feature of Kotlin. Extension functions allow us to add the functions in the native class sets. All extension functions are statically resolved. Check out `DateExtension.kt`, it has three extension functions written for `Long` objects. They return different date formats. The code inside it may look a bit strange, which we will discuss in the following section:

```
fun Long.getShortDate(): String {
    val getFormattedDate: dynamic = js("window.getShortDate")
    return getFormattedDate(this)
}

fun Long.getFullDate(): String {
    val getFormattedDate: dynamic = js("window.getFullDate")
    return getFormattedDate(this)
}

fun Long.getFullWeekDay(): String {
    val getFormattedDate: dynamic = js("window.getFullWeekDay")
    return getFormattedDate(this)
}
```

We don't need to write utility methods in Kotlin. We should prefer extension functions over `Utils`. Do not try to have any heavy methods as extension functions, instance functions are always good.

Writing extension functions to format dates and to have some validation functions is OK. But it's not good to write an API calling function for any string class. Remember they are statically resolved. A project loaded with static is not good for memory.

Giving final touches

We wrote many lines of code so far. We also refactored them periodically. Once again it's a time to refactor and look for the possible improvements. Let's take a look back and see if there is any possibility of refactoring the code further.

Adding CSS

Let's add some custom font and style some of the missed HTML elements. We have used Robot font, you can use any font of your desire.

It's a simple one-liner code to mention the font in the app. Add the following line to your `index.html` page just after the `<body>` tag:

```
<link href="https://fonts.googleapis.com/css?
  family=Roboto+Condensed" rel="stylesheet">
```

And in `main.css` apply the font to an entire HTML page:

```
html *
{
   font-family: 'Roboto Condensed', sans-serif;
}
```

Reload the page. Looks beautiful now, doesn't it?

Interoperability with JavaScript

After all the hard work we did to develop Kotlin code, what if we have a very crucial code well written, well tested, but written in JavaScript. Are we going to convert it into Kotlin? No. The way Kotlin code can interoperate with Java, Kotlin for JavaScript is interoperable with JavaScript. This means JavaScript can call Kotlin code and Kotlin can call JavaScript code.

We have covered this as well. Kotlin does not have a `Date` class that can accept a date in UTC format, but JavaScript has. We will format our dates in JavaScript and Kotlin will call those functions.

We wrote three functions in our `index.html` file just inside a `<script>` tag and preceding the Kotlin `<script>` tags. The sequence does matter here! Consider the following code snippet:

```
<script>
  window.getShortDate = function(longDate) {
    var options={month:'long', day:'numeric'};
    return new Date(longDate*1000).toLocaleDateString('en-
    US',options);
  }

  window.getFullWeekDay = function(longDate) {
    var options={weekday:'long'};
    return new Date(longDate*1000).toLocaleDateString('en-
    US',options);
  }

  window.getFullDate = function(longDate) {
    var options={weekday:'long', day:'numeric',
    month:'long',year:'numeric'};
    return new Date(longDate*1000).toLocaleDateString('en-
    US',options);
  }
</script>
```

We are adding functions as global level functions by putting them as a part of the window. You can inline some JavaScript code into your Kotlin code using the `js("...")` function. Now having a look at the `DateExtension.kt` will make more sense:

```
fun Long.getShortDate(): String {
    val getFormattedDate: dynamic = js("window.getShortDate")
    return getFormattedDate(this)
}

fun Long.getFullDate(): String {
    val getFormattedDate: dynamic = js("window.getFullDate")
    return getFormattedDate(this)
}

fun Long.getFullWeekDay(): String {
    val getFormattedDate: dynamic = js("window.getFullWeekDay")
    return getFormattedDate(this)
}
```

Each function is giving a call to a JavaScript function using a `js("...")` function.

You should observe a keyword dynamic. It means you are throwing away all the advantages of Kotlin being statically typed and taking a risk to resolve anything that is returned from the `js` function. Nothing wrong with it, but use it carefully.

Summary

We are sure you had a fantastic ride with us for this chapter. We learned the basics to the advanced elements such as setting up Kotlin for JavaScript projects, interacting with DOM elements, DSL, interoperability, and so on.

The purpose of this chapter was to show that Kotlin's support for JavaScript is no more an experiment. It's already production ready. You can see what can be done using the benefits of statically typed programming languages and powerful JavaScript ecosystems.

The app is written using Kotlin version 1.1.4 . However, keep in mind that Kotlin is evolving rapidly. There are a lot of other topics where Kotlin is capable working with strongly typed libraries such as jQuery, working with modules and using ts2kt for dealing with libraries.

In the next chapter, we have a more interesting topic, that is, using Kotlin code to write Node.js applications. We promise that the upcoming ride is even more exciting and full of learning and fun.

5

Chat Application with Server-Side JavaScript Generation

So far, we have seen Kotlin in action with Spring Boot, Android, and JavaScript client side. When one mentions server-side JavaScript technology, Node.js is what comes to our mind first. Node.js is an extremely powerful and robust platform. Using this JavaScript platform, we can build server-side applications very easily. One cannot doubt the capabilities of this platform when a giant like Google is running a great Firebase service on the node. It has become the platform of choice to build REST APIs, chatbots, and many more backend services. The primary appeal is that developers can use the same skill set web side and server side too.

Now, Kotlin is a modern language and is gaining popularity in the JavaScript community day by day. The Kotlin language has many modern features and is statically typed; hence, it is superior to JavaScript. Just like JavaScript, developers that know Kotlin can use the same language skills on both sides (in fact, they can work on more platforms than those that JavaScript dominates), but, they also have the advantage of using a better language. As Kotlin is being statically typed, the IDE is better able chance to provide facilities such as auto-suggestions. The Kotlin code gets transpiled to JavaScript and that in turns works with the Node.js. This is the mechanism that lets you use the Kotlin code to work with a server-side technology, such as Node.js.

In this chapter, we will focus on creating a chat application that uses Kotlin by using the Node.js technology. So, basically, we will be transpiling Kotlin code to JavaScript on the server side. We will learn the following topics in this chapter:

- Setting up a Node.js project using Kotlin
- Creating a basic project where the Kotlin code is transpiled into the Node.js code
- Making a chat application using Socket.IO, entirely written in Kotlin
- Making a client/browser-side JavaScript, entirely written in Kotlin

Creating our first Node.js app using Kotlin

This will be real fun. Like the previous JavaScript chapter, we would like to separate our basic setup and project creation. These steps require us to be extra cautious.

Choosing an IDE

Node.js is a very popular JavaScript Framework. It's been very well supported by different IDEs, such as WebStorm, Cloud 9, Eclipse, Komodo, and so on. All of them have built-in features that a developer requires to build the Node.js app. However, we cannot choose most of these IDEs (remember, we need an IDE that supports Kotlin). We will have to go with IntelliJ IDEA Ultimate, which supports both Kotlin and Node.JS (via plugin). Just install it from `https://www.jetbrains.com/idea`, and you are all set to create your first Node.js project using Kotlin.

Installing Node.js

Installing Node.js is pretty straightforward. Go to `https://nodejs.org/en/download/` and choose an appropriate OS and platform that is applicable to you. Once you have successfully installed Node.js, verify that you both the node and the **npm** (**node package manager**) are working properly. Execute the following commands and verify the output.

To check the node version, execute the following command:

```
node -v
```

To check the npm version, execute the following command:

```
npm -v
```

You will have an output somewhat similar to the following screenshot:

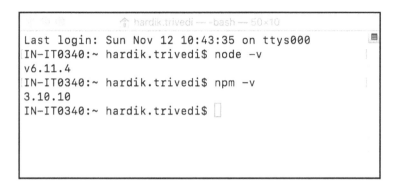

```
Last login: Sun Nov 12 10:43:35 on ttys000
IN-IT0340:~ hardik.trivedi$ node -v
v6.11.4
IN-IT0340:~ hardik.trivedi$ npm -v
3.10.10
IN-IT0340:~ hardik.trivedi$
```

Installing the Node.js plugin

Follow these steps to install the NodeJS plugin:

1. Open IntelliJ IDEA Ultimate.
2. Go to **Preferences** | **Plugins** | **Install JetBrains Plugin**.
3. Search for NodeJS.
4. Click on **Install**.
5. Restart your IDE so that installed changes will be applied.

You can refer to the following screenshot to help you to identify the correct plugin:

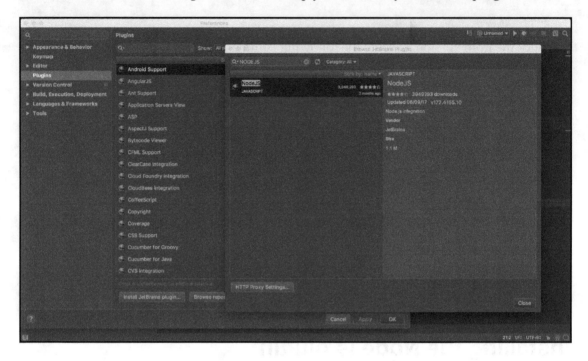

Creating a project

We will create a Gradle project first. Read more about getting started with Kotlin and JavaScript with Gradle at `https://kotlinlang.org/docs/tutorials/javascript/getting-started-gradle/getting-started-with-gradle.html`. We will guide you through the steps to create a simple Gradle project. The final outcome of this project will display a welcome message on the browser using Kotlin code; just follow these steps:

1. Create a Gradle project. Make sure you select only **Kotlin (JavaScript)** from the option and click on **Next**, as shown in the following screenshot:

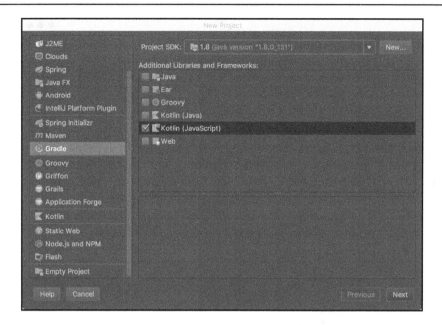

2. Give **GroupId** as `KotlinBlueprints` and **ArtifactId** as `hello_kotlin_node`, and then click on **Next**, as shown in the following screenshot:

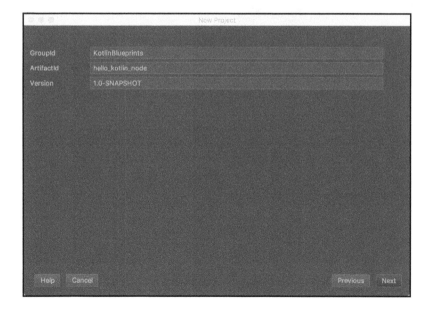

3. Uncheck the **Create separate module per source set** option, but do select the **Use default gradle wrapper (recommended)** option, and click on **Next**. We are selecting the default Gradle wrapper so that when someone wants to use your project, it will run even if that machine does not have Gradle installed. We unchecked the **source set options** because that is something we do not want right now. It's for targeting different code base based on product flavors. It's a logical grouping of your code.

4. Perform the final steps. Do nothing in this window. All fields will be shown as prepopulated. Simply click on the **Finish** option. IDEA Ultimate will create a project with required the Gradle files. Check your directory; it will have `build.gradle`, the `settings.gradle` files, and the `gradle` folder generated. The `build.gradle` file is the key file that has all the information that is required to build a project, as shown in the following screenshot:

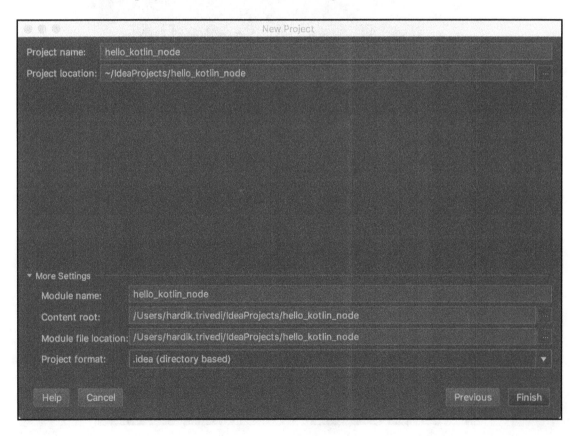

5. Now it's time to initialize the project with the node. We will let this project know that it will use the node. Execute the following command on the Terminal (move to your root of the project directory first). The npm is a utility to manage dependencies for the node, and the following command is used to initialize npm:

```
npm init
```

6. Install the Kotlin dependency. Our project is based on Kotlin, and we need the Kotlin dependency to be there before we build the project. Execute the following command on Terminal:

```
npm install kotlin --save
```

7. Add the ExpressJS Framework so that we will have a basic set of libraries to play with Node.js, as shown in the following command:

```
npm install express --save
```

8. Now comes the crucial step; we will create a Kotlin file. Inside src/main/kotlin, create Main.kt. Our Main.kt will look like the following:

```
external fun require(module:String):dynamic

fun main(args: Array<String>) {

  val express = require("express")
  val app = express()

  app.get("/", { request, response ->
   response.type("text/plain")
  response.send("Hello! Kotlin Blueprints team, welcomes you to
   the Node.js demo.")
  })

  app.listen(3000, {
    println("Listening to request on port 3000")
  })
}
```

9. Let's take some time and find out what this code says. We are saying that our Kotlin file is using an external require function, which will take a string as a parameter, so we will use the following line of code:

```
external fun require(module:String):dynamic
```

10. The dynamic keyword has a meaning. Kotlin is statically typed, because of interoperability features, it still has to deal with untyped or loosely typed languages and environments. This allows you to call any property or function on any type of object. It basically turns off Kotlin's type checker. We will require an express library, so we will need to use the following command:

```
require("express")
```

The `app.get()` method says that when a user lands on the page, we need to display a welcome message, and that `app.listen` should listen for any request on port `3000`.

11. Specify output options to Gradle. When we build our project, we want the Gradle build script to know where to generate the output `.js` file. We want our Kotlin code to be compiled and to generate an `app.js` output file inside the `node_js` directory. The Gradle reads your `build.gradle` file while creating a build, so the following information will go in your `build.gradle` file. Your `build.gradle` file should look like the following piece of code—the part that is highlighted in bold is the section that you have to add:

```
group 'KotlinBlueprints'
version '1.0-SNAPSHOT'

buildscript {
  ext.kotlin_version = '1.1.4-3'

  repositories {
    mavenCentral()
  }
  dependencies {
    classpath "org.jetbrains.kotlin:kotlin-gradle-
    plugin:$kotlin_version"
  }
}

apply plugin: 'kotlin2js'

repositories {
  mavenCentral()
}

dependencies {
  compile "org.jetbrains.kotlin:kotlin-stdlib-
    js:$kotlin_version"
```

```
    }

compileKotlin2Js {
    kotlinOptions.moduleKind = "commonjs"
    kotlinOptions.outputFile = "node_js/app.js"
    kotlinOptions.sourceMap = true
}
```

12. Compile the Kotlin code using Gradle. The following command will download Gradle files on its first execution. Sit back and wait for the download to complete; it may take few minutes:

    `./gradlew build`

13. Start the node server and verify the output. Start your server by accessing `http://localhost:3000`, and you should see the following output:

    `node node_js/app.js`

The following screenshot represents the node server on the local host:

Damn, you are good. Congratulations, you have successfully converted your Kotlin code into a Node.js code. In the next section, we will take a deeper look into Kotlin and its Node.js support.

Creating a chat application

In the previous section, we saw how we can configure Kotlin so that it can be used with Node.js. We also created our first Node.js app using Kotlin. Now, it's time to take a deep dive into Kotlin and build a bigger app. Our chat app will have following functionalities:

- User can log in by entering their nickname
- User can see the list of online users
- User will get notified when a new user joins

- User can receive chats from anyone
- User can perform a group chat in a chat room
- User will receive a notification when any user leaves the chat

To visualize the app we will be developing, take a look at the following screenshots.

The following screenshot is a page where the user will enter a nickname and gain an entry in our chat app:

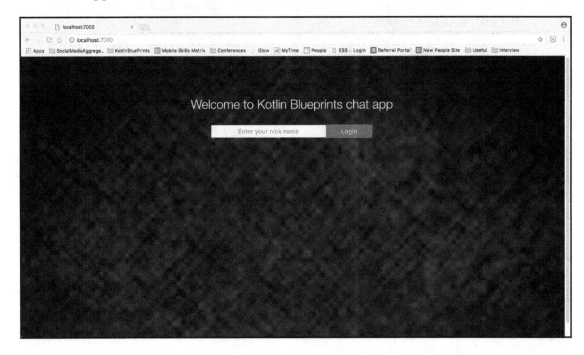

In the following screen, you can see a chat window and a list of online users:

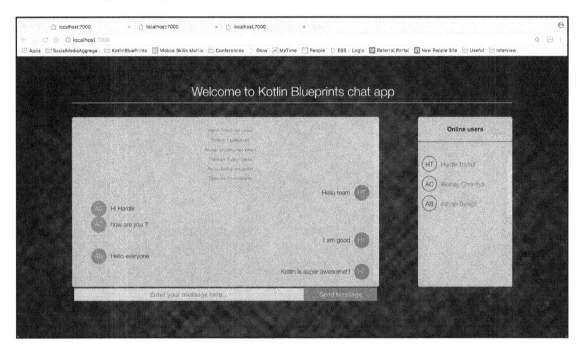

We have slightly configured this application in a different way. We have kept the backend code module and frontend code module separate using the following method:

1. Create a new project named `kotlin_node_chat_app` by following the steps that we performed in the previous section.
2. Now, create a new Gradle module named `backend` and select **Kotlin (JavaScript)** under the libraries and additional information window, and follow the remaining steps.
3. Similarly, also create a Gradle module named `webapp`.

The `backend` module will contain all the Kotlin code that will be converted into Node.JS code later, and the `webapp` module will contain all the Kotlin code that will later be converted into the JavaScript code. We have referred to the directory structure from `https://github.com/techprd/kotlin_node_js_seed`.

After performing the previous steps correctly, your project will have three `build.gradle` files. We have highlighted all three files in the project explorer section, as shown in the following screenshot:

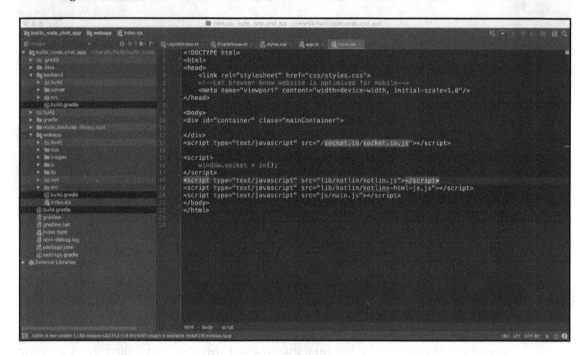

Setting up the Node.js server

We need to initialize our root directory for the node. Execute `npm init` and it will create `package.json`. Now our login page is created. To run it, we need to set up the Node.js server. We want to create the server in such a way that by executing `npm start`, it should start the server.

To achieve it, our `package.json` file should look like the following piece of code:

```
{
    "name": "kotlin_node_chat_app",
    "version": "1.0.0",
    "description": "",
    "main": "backend/server/app.js",
    "scripts": {
      "start": "node backend/server/app.js"
    },
  "author": "Hardik Trivedi",
  "license": "ISC",
  "dependencies": {
      "ejs": "^2.5.7",
      "express": "^4.16.2",
      "kotlin": "^1.1.60",
      "socket.io": "^2.0.4"
  }
}
```

We have specified a few dependencies here as well:

- EJS to render HTML pages
- Express.JS as its framework, which makes it easier to deal with Node.js
- Kotlin, because, ultimately, we want to write our code into Kotlin and want it compiled into the Node.js code
- Socket.IO to perform chat

Execute `npm install` on the Terminal/Command Prompt and it should trigger the download of all these dependencies.

Specifying the output files

Now, it's very important where your output will be generated once you trigger the build. For that, `build.gradle` will help us. Specify the following lines in your module-level `build.gradle` file.

The `backend` module's `build.gradle` will have the following lines of code:

```
compileKotlin2Js {
  kotlinOptions.outputFile = "${projectDir}/server/app.js"
  kotlinOptions.moduleKind = "commonjs"
  kotlinOptions.sourceMap = true
}
```

The `webapp` module's `build.gradle` will have the following lines of code:

```
compileKotlin2Js {
    kotlinOptions.metaInfo = true
    kotlinOptions.outputFile = "${projectDir}/js/main.js"
    kotlinOptions.sourceMap = true
    kotlinOptions.main = "call"
}
```

In both the `compileKotlin2Js` nodes, `kotlinOptions.outputFile` plays a key role. This basically tells us that once Kotlin's code gets compiled, it will generate `app.js` and `main.js` for Node.js and JavaScript respectively.

In the `index.ejs` file, you should define a script tag to load `main.js`. It will look something like the following line of code:

```
<script type="text/javascript" src="js/main.js"></script>
```

Along with this, also specify the following two tags:

```
<script type="text/javascript" src="lib/kotlin/kotlin.js"></script>
<script type="text/javascript" src="lib/kotlin/kotlinx-html-js.js">
  </script>
```

Examining the compilation output

The `kotlin.js` and `kotlinx-html-js.js` files are nothing but the Kotlin output files. It's not compilation output, but actually transpiled output. The following are output compilations:

- `kotlin.js`: This is the runtime and standard library. It doesn't change between applications, and it's tied to the version of Kotlin being used.
- `{module}.js`: This is the actual code from the application. All files are compiled into a single JavaScript file that has the same name as the module.
- `{file}.meta.js`: This metafile will be used for reflection and other functionalities.

Let's assume our final `Main.kt` file will look like this:

```
fun main(args: Array<String>) {

    val socket: dynamic = js("window.socket")

    val chatWindow = ChatWindow {
```

```
    println("here")
    socket.emit("new_message", it)
  }

  val loginWindow = LoginWindow {
    chatWindow.showChatWindow(it)
    socket.emit("add_user", it)
  }
  loginWindow.showLogin()


  socket.on("login", { data ->
   chatWindow.showNewUserJoined(data)
   chatWindow.showOnlineUsers(data)
  })

  socket.on("user_joined", { data ->
   chatWindow.showNewUserJoined(data)
   chatWindow.addNewUsers(data)
  })

  socket.on("user_left", { data ->
   chatWindow.showUserLeft(data)
  })

  socket.on("new_message", { data ->
   chatWindow.showNewMessage(data)
  })
}
```

For this, inside `main.js`, our main function will look like this:

```
function main(args) {
  var socket = window.socket;
  var chatWindow = new ChatWindow(main$lambda(socket));
  var loginWindow = new LoginWindow(main$lambda_0(chatWindow,
   socket));
  loginWindow.showLogin();
  socket.on('login', main$lambda_1(chatWindow));
  socket.on('user_joined', main$lambda_2(chatWindow));
  socket.on('user_left', main$lambda_3(chatWindow));
  socket.on('new_message', main$lambda_4(chatWindow));
}
```

The actual `main.js` file will be much more bulky because it will have all the code transpiled, including other functions and `LoginWindow` and `ChatWindow` classes. Keep a watchful eye on how the Lambda functions are converted into simple JavaScript functions. Lambda functions, for all socket events, are transpiled into the following piece of code:

```
function main$lambda_1(closure$chatWindow) {
  return function (data) {
    closure$chatWindow.showNewUserJoined_qk3xy8$(data);
    closure$chatWindow.showOnlineUsers_qk3xy8$(data);
  };
}
function main$lambda_2(closure$chatWindow) {
  return function (data) {
    closure$chatWindow.showNewUserJoined_qk3xy8$(data);
    closure$chatWindow.addNewUsers_qk3xy8$(data);
   };
}
function main$lambda_3(closure$chatWindow) {
  return function (data) {
    closure$chatWindow.showUserLeft_qk3xy8$(data);
  };
}
function main$lambda_4(closure$chatWindow) {
  return function (data) {
    closure$chatWindow.showNewMessage_qk3xy8$(data);
  };
}
```

As can be seen, Kotlin aims to create very concise and readable JavaScript, allowing us to interact with it as needed.

Specifying the router

We need to write a behavior in the `route.kt` file. This will let the server know which page to load when any request hits the server. The `router.kt` file will look like this:

```
fun router() {
  val express = require("express")
  val router = express.Router()


  router.get("/", { req, res ->
   res.render("index")
  })
```

```
      return router
    }
```

This simply means that whenever a `get` request with no name approaches the server, it should display an index page to the user. We are told to instruct the framework to refer to the `router.kt` file by writing the following line of code:

```
app.use("/", router())
```

Starting the node server

Now let's create a server. We should create an `app.kt` file under the `backend` module at the `backend/src/kotlin` path. Refer to the source code to verify. Write the following piece of code in `app.kt`:

```kotlin
external fun require(module: String): dynamic

external val process: dynamic
external val __dirname: dynamic

fun main(args: Array<String>) {

  println("Server Starting!")

  val express = require("express")
  val app = express()
  val path = require("path")

  val http = require("http")
  /**
   * Get port from environment and store in Express.
   */
  val port = normalizePort(process.env.PORT)
  app.set("port", port)

  // view engine setup
  app.set("views", path.join(__dirname, "../../webapp"))
  app.set("view engine", "ejs")
  app.use(express.static("webapp"))

  val server = http.createServer(app)

  app.use("/", router())

  app.listen(port, {
    println("Chat app listening on port http://localhost:$port")
```

```
    })
  }

  fun normalizePort(port: Int) = if (port >= 0) port else 7000
```

These are multiple things to highlight here:

- `external`: This is basically an indicator for Kotlin that the line written along with this a pure JavaScript code. Also, when this code gets compiled into the respected language, the compiler understands that the class, function, or property written along with that will be provided by the developer, and so no JavaScript code should be generated for that invocation. The `external` modifier is automatically applied to nested declarations. For example, consider the following code block. We declare the class as `external` and automatically all its functions and properties are treated as `external`:

```
external class Node {
  val firstChild: Node

  fun append(child: Node): Node

  fun removeChild(child: Node): Node

  // etc
}
```

- `dynamic`: You will often see the usage of `dynamic` while working with JavaScript. Kotlin is a statically typed language, but it still has to interoperate with languages such as JavaScript. To support such use cases with a loosely or untyped programming language, `dynamic` is useful. It turns off Kotlin's type checker.
  A value of this type can be assigned to any variable or passed anywhere as a parameter.

  Any value can be assigned to a variable of `dynamic` type or passed to a function that takes `dynamic` as a parameter. Null checks are disabled for such values.

- `require("express")`: We typically use ExpressJS with Node.js. It's a framework that goes hand in hand with Node.js. It's designed with the sole purpose of developing web applications. A Node.js developer must be very familiar with it.

- `process.env.PORT`: This will find an available port on the server, as simple as that. This line is required if you want to deploy your application on a utility like Heroku. Also, notice the `normalizePort` function. See how concise it is. The `if...else` condition is written as an expression. No explicit `return` keyword is required. Kotlin compiler also identifies that `if (port >= 0) port else 7000` will always return `Int`, hence no explicit `return` type is required. Smart, isn't it!

- `__dirname`: This is always a location where your currently executing script is present. We will use it to create a path to indicate where we have kept our web pages.
- `app.listen()`: This is a crucial one. It starts the socket and listens for the incoming request. It takes multiple parameters. Mainly, we will use two parameterized functions, that take the port number and connection `callback` as an argument. The `app.listen()` method is identical to `http.Server.listen()`. In Kotlin, it takes a Lambda function.

Now, it's time to kick-start the server. Hit the Gradle by using `./gradlew build`. All Kotlin code will get compiled into Node.js code. On Terminal, go to the root directory and execute `npm start`. You should be able to see the following message on your Terminal/Command Prompt:

```
:webapp:compileKotlin2Js
w: /Users/hardik.trivedi/Hardik/Packt/kotlin_node_chat_app/webapp/src/main/kotlin/views/ChatWindow.kt: (66, 29): Uncheck
ed cast: Any? to Array<String>
w: /Users/hardik.trivedi/Hardik/Packt/kotlin_node_chat_app/webapp/src/main/kotlin/views/ChatWindow.kt: (114, 28): Parame
ter 'data' is never used
w: /Users/hardik.trivedi/Hardik/Packt/kotlin_node_chat_app/webapp/src/main/kotlin/views/ChatWindow.kt: (119, 17): Variab
le 'element' is never used
:webapp:processResources NO-SOURCE
:webapp:classes
:webapp:jar
:webapp:assemble
:webapp:compileTestJava NO-SOURCE
:webapp:compileTestKotlin2Js NO-SOURCE
:webapp:processTestResources NO-SOURCE
:webapp:testClasses UP-TO-DATE
:webapp:test NO-SOURCE
:webapp:check UP-TO-DATE
:webapp:build

BUILD SUCCESSFUL

Total time: 9.687 secs
IN-IT0340:kotlin_node_chat_app hardik.trivedi$ npm start

> kotlin_node_chat_app@1.0.0 start /Users/hardik.trivedi/Hardik/Packt/kotlin_node_chat_app
> node backend/server/app.js

Server Starting!
Chat app listening on port http://localhost:7000
```

Creating a login page

Now, let's begin with the login page. Along with that, we will have to enable some other settings in the project as well. If you refer to a screenshots that we mentioned at the beginning of the previous section, you can make out that we will have the title, the input filed, and a button as a part of the login page. We will create the page using Kotlin and the entire HTML tree structure, and by applying CSS to them, the will be part of our Kotlin code. For that, you should refer to the `Main.kt` and `LoginWindow` files.

Creating an index.ejs file

We will use **EJS (effective JavaScript templating)** to render HTML content on the page. EJS and Node.js go hand in hand. It's simple, flexible, easy to debug, and increases development speed. Initially, `index.ejs` would look like the following code snippet:

```
<!DOCTYPE html>
<html>
<head>
    <meta name="viewport" content="width=device-width, initial-
    scale=1.0"/>
</head>

<body>
<div id="container" class="mainContainer">

</div>
</body>
</html>
```

The `<div>` tag will contain all different views, for example, the Login View, Chat Window View, and so on.

Using DSL

DSL stands for domain-specific language. As the name indicates, it gives you the feeling as if you are writing code in a language using terminology particular to a given domain without being geeky, but then, this terminology is cleverly embedded as a syntax in a powerful language. If you are from the Groovy community, you must be aware of builders. Groovy builders allow you to define data in a semi-declarative way. It's a kind of mini-language of its own. Builders are considered good for generating XML and laying out UI components. The Kotlin DSL uses Lambdas a lot.

The DSL in Kotlin is a type-safe builder. It means we can detect compilation errors in IntelliJ's beautiful IDE. The type-check builders are much better than the dynamically typed builders of Groovy.

Using kotlinx.html

The DSL to build HTML trees is a pluggable dependency. We therefore need to set it up and configure it for our project. We are using Gradle as a build tool and Gradle has the best way to manage the dependencies. We will define the following line of code in our `build.gradle` file to use `kotlinx.html`:

```
compile("org.jetbrains.kotlinx:kotlinx-html-js:$html_version")
```

Gradle will automatically download this dependency from `jcenter()`. Build your project from menu **Build | Build Project**. You can also trigger a build from the terminal/command prompt. To build a project from the Terminal, go to the root directory of your project and then execute `./gradlew build`.

Now create the `index.ejs` file under the `webapp` directory. At this moment, your `index.ejs` file may look like the following:

Inside your `LoginWindow` class file, you should write the following piece of code:

```
class LoginWindow(val callback: (String) -> Unit) {

  fun showLogin() {
    val formContainer = document.getElementById("container") as
      HTMLDivElement
    val loginDiv = document.create.div {
      id = "loginDiv"
      h3(classes = "title") {
        +"Welcome to Kotlin Blueprints chat app"
      }
      input(classes = "nickNameInput") {
        id = "nickName"
        onInputFunction = onInput()
        maxLength = 16.toString()
        placeholder = "Enter your nick name"
      }
      button(classes = "loginButton") {
        +"Login"
          onClickFunction = onLoginButtonClicked()
      }
    }
```

```
        formContainer.appendChild(loginDiv)
    }
}
```

Observe how we have provided the ID, input types, and a default ZIP code value. A default ZIP code value is optional. Let's spend some time understanding the previous code. The `div`, `input`, `button`, and `h3` all these are nothing but functions. They are basically Lambda functions.

The following are the functions that use Lambda as the last parameter. You can call them in different ways:

```
someFunction({})

someFunction("KotlinBluePrints",1,{})

someFunction("KotlinBluePrints",1){}

someFunction{}
```

Lambda functions

Lambda functions are nothing but functions without a name. We used to call them anonymous functions. A function is basically passed into a parameter of a function call, but as an expression. They are very useful. They save us a lot of time by not writing specific functions in an abstract class or interface.

Lambda usage can be as simple the following code snippet, where it seems like we are simply binding a block an invocation of the `helloKotlin` function:

```
fun main(args: Array<String>) {
  val helloKotlin={println("Hello from KotlinBlueprints team!")}
  helloKotlin()
}
```

At the same time, lambda can be a bit complex as well, just like the following code block:

```
fun <T> lock(lock: Lock, body: () -> T): T {
  lock.lock()
  try {
    return body()
  }
  finally {
    lock.unlock()
```

```
      }
   }
```

In the previous function, we are acquiring a lock before executing a function and releasing it when the function gets executed. This way, you can synchronously call a function in a multithreaded environment. So, if we have a use case where we want to execute `sharedObject.someCrucialFunction()` in a thread-safe environment, we will call the preceding lock function like this:

```
lock(lock,{sharedObject.someCrucialFunction()})
```

Now, the lambda function is the last parameter of a function call, so it can be easily written like this:

```
lock(lock) {
   sharedObject.someCrucialFunction()
}
```

Look how expressive and easy to understand the code is. We will dig more into the Lambda in the upcoming section.

Reading the nickname

In the `index.ejs` page, we will have an input field with the ID `nickName` when it is rendered. We can simply read the value by writing the following lines of code:

```
val nickName = (document.getElementById("nickName") as?
  HTMLInputElement)?.value
```

However, to cover more possibilities, we have written it in a slightly different way. We have written it as if we are taking the input as an event.

The following code block will continuously read the value that is entered into the `nickName` input field:

```
private fun onInput(): (Event) -> Unit {
  return {
    val input = it.currentTarget as HTMLInputElement
    when (input.id) {
      "nickName" -> nickName = input.value
      "emailId" -> email = input.value
    }
  }
}
```

Check out, we have used the `when` function, which is a replacement for the `switch` case. The preceding code will check whether the ID of the element is `nickName` or `emailId`, and, based on that, it will assign the value to the respective objects by reading them from the in-out field. In the app, we will only have the nickname as the input file, but using the preceding approach, you can read the value from multiple input fields.

In its simplest form, it looks like this:

```
when (x) {
    1 -> print ("x == 1")
    2 -> print ("x == 2")
    else -> { // Note the block
      print ("x is neither 1 nor 2")
    }
}
```

The `when` function compares its argument against all branches, top to bottom, until some branch condition is met. The `when` function can be used either as an expression or as a statement.

The `else` branch is evaluated if none of the other branch conditions are satisfied. If `when` is used as an expression, the `else` branch is mandatory, unless the compiler can prove that all possible cases are covered with branch conditions.

If many cases should be handled in the same way, the branch conditions may be combined with a comma, as shown in the following code:

```
when (x) {
    0, 1 -> print ("x == 0 or x == 1")
    else -> print ("otherwise")
}
```

The following uses arbitrary expressions (not only constants) as branch conditions:

```
when (x) {
    parseInt (s) -> print ("s encodes x")
    else -> print ("s does not encode x")
}
```

The following is used to check a value for being `in` or `!in` a range or a collection:

```
when (x) {
    in 1..10 -> print ("x is in the range")
    in validNumbers -> print ("x is valid")
    !in 10..20 -> print ("x is outside the range")
    else -> print ("none of the above")
}
```

Passing nickname to the server

Once our setup is done, we are able to start the server and see the login page. It's time to pass the nickname or server and enter the chat room.

We have written a function named `onLoginButtonClicked()`. The body for this function should like this:

```
private fun onLoginButtonClicked(): (Event) -> Unit {
    return {
      if (!nickName.isBlank()) {
          val formContainer = document.getElementById("loginDiv") as
           HTMLDivElement
          formContainer.remove()
          callback(nickName)
      }
    }
}
```

The preceding function does two special things:

- Smart casting
- Registering a simple `callback`

Smart cast

Unlike any other programming language, Kotlin also provides class cast support. The `document.getElementById()` method returns an `Element` type `if` instance. We basically want it to cast into `HTMLDivElement` to perform some `<div>` related operation. So, using `as`, we cast the `Element` into `HTMLDivElement`.

With the `as` keyword, it's unsafe casting. It's always better to use `as?`. On a successful cast, it will give an instance of that class; otherwise it returns `null`. So, while using `as?`, you have to use Kotlin's null safety feature. This gives your app a great safety net `onLoginButtonClicked` can be refactored by modifying the code a bit. The following code block is the modified version of the function. We have highlighted the modification in bold:

```
private fun onLoginButtonClicked(): (Event) -> Unit {
    return {
      if (!nickName.isBlank()) {
          val formContainer = document.getElementById("loginDiv") as?
           HTMLDivElement
          formContainer?.remove()
```

```
        callback(nickName)
     }
  }
}
```

Registering a callback

Oftentimes, we need a function to notify us when something gets done. We prefer
`callbacks` in JavaScript. To write a click event for a button, a typical JavaScript code could
look like the following:

```
$("#btn_submit").click(function() {
  alert("Submit Button Clicked");
});
```

With Kotlin, it's simple. Kotlin uses the Lambda function to achieve this. For
the `LoginWindow` class, we have passed a `callback` as a constructor parameter. In the
`LoginWindow` class (`val callback: (String) -> Unit`), the class header specifies that
the constructor will take a `callback` as a parameter, which will return a string when
invoked.

To pass a `callback`, we will write the following line of code:

```
callback(nickName)
```

To consume a `callback`, we will write code that will look like this:

```
val loginWindow = LoginWindow {
  chatWindow.showChatWindow(it)
  socket.emit("add_user", it)
}
```

So, when `callback(nickName)` is called, `chatWindow.showChatWindow` will get called
and the nickname will be passed. Without it, you are accessing nothing but the nickname.

Establishing a socket connection

We shall be using the `Socket.IO` library to set up sockets between the server and the
clients. `Socket.IO` takes care of the following complexities:

- Setting up connections
- Sending and receiving messages to multiple clients
- Notifying clients when the connection is disconnected

Read more about `Socket.IO` at `https://socket.io/`.

Setting up Socket.IO

We have already specified the dependency for `Socket.IO` in our `package.json` file. Look at this file. It has a dependency block, which is mentioned in the following code block:

```
"dependencies": {
  "ejs": "^2.5.7",
  "express": "^4.16.2",
  "kotlin": "^1.1.60",
  "socket.io": "^2.0.4"
}
```

When we perform `npm install`, it basically downloads the `socket-io.js` file and keeps `node_modules | socket.io` inside.

We will add this JavaScript file to our `index.ejs` file.

There we can find the following mentioned `<script>` tag inside the `<body>` tag:

```
<script type="text/javascript" src="/socket.io/socket.io.js">
  </script>
```

Also, initialize `socket` in the same `index.js` file like this:

```
<script>
  window.socket = io();
</script>
```

Listening to events

With the `Socket.IO` library, you should open a port and listen to the request using the following lines of code. Initially, we were directly using `app.listen()`, but now, we will pass that function as a listener for `sockets`:

```
val io = require("socket.io").listen(app.listen(port, {
  println("Chat app listening on port http://localhost:$port")
}))
```

The server will listen to the following events and based on those events, it will perform certain tasks:

- Listen to the successful socket connection with the client
- Listen for the new user login events
- Whenever a new user joins the chat, add it to the online users chat list and broadcast it to every client so that they will know that a new member has joined the chat
- Listen to the request when someone sends a message
- Receive the message and broadcast it to all the clients so that the client can receive it and show it in the chat window

Emitting the event

The `Socket.IO` library works on a simple principle—emit and listen. Clients emit the messages and a listener listens to those messages and performs an action associated with them.

So now, whenever a user successfully logs in, we will emit an event named `add_user` and the server will add it to an online user's list.

The following code line emits the message:

```
socket.emit("add_user", it)
```

The following code snippet listens to the message and adds a user to the list:

```
socket.on("add_user", { nickName ->
  socket.nickname= nickName
  numOfUsers = numOfUsers.inc()
  usersList.add(nickName as String)
})
```

The `socket.on` function will listen to the `add_user` event and store the nickname in the socket.

Incrementing and decrementing operator overloading

There are a lot of things operator overloading can do, and we have used quite a few features here. Check out how we increment a count of online users:

```
numOfUsers = numOfUsers.inc()
```

It is a much more readable code compared to `numOfUsers = numOfUsers+1`, `umOfUsers += 1`, or `numOfUsers++`.

Similarly, we can decrement any number by using the `dec()` function.

Operator overloading applies to the whole set of unary operators, increment-decrement operators, binary operators, and index access operator. Read more about all of them at `https://kotlinlang.org/docs/reference/operator-overloading.html`.

Showing a list of online users

Now we need to show the list of online users. For this, we need to pass the list of all online users and the count of users along with it.

Using the data class

The `data` class is one of the most popular features among Kotlin developers. It is similar to the concept of the `Model` class.

The compiler automatically derives the following members from all properties declared in the primary constructor:

- The `equals()`/`hashCode()` pair
- The `toString()` of the `User(name=John, age=42)` form
- The `componentN()` functions corresponding to the properties in their order of declaration
- The `copy()` function

A simple version of the `data` class can look like the following line of code, where `name` and `age` will become properties of a class:

```
data class User(val name: String, val age: Int)
```

With this single line and, mainly, with the **data** keyword, you get `equals()`/`hasCode()`, `toString()` and the benefits of getters and setters by using `val/var` in the form of properties. What a powerful keyword!

Using the Pair class

In our app, we have chosen the `Pair` class to demonstrate its usage. The `Pair` is also a `data` class. Consider the following line of code:

```
data class Pair<out A, out B> : Serializable
```

It represents a generic pair of two values. You can look at it as a key–value utility in the form of a class. We need to create a JSON object of a number of online users with the list of their nicknames. You can create a JSON object with the help of a `Pair` class. Take a look at the following lines of code:

```
val userJoinedData = json(Pair("numOfUsers", numOfUsers),
  Pair("nickname", nickname), Pair("usersList", usersList))
```

The preceding JSON object will look like the following piece of code in the JSON format:

```
{
  "numOfUsers": 3,
  "nickname": "Hardik Trivedi",
  "usersList": [
    "Hardik Trivedi",
    "Akshay Chordiya",
    "Ashish Belagali"
  ]
}
```

Iterating list

The user's list that we have passed inside the JSON object will be iterated and rendered on the page. Kotlin has a variety of ways to iterate over the list. Actually, anything that implements iterable can be represented as a sequence of elements that can be iterated. It has a lot of utility functions, some of which are mentioned in the following list:

- `hasNext()`: This returns true if the iteration has more elements
- `hasPrevious()`: This returns true if there are elements in the iteration before the current element
- `next()`: This returns the next element in the iteration
- `nextIndex()`: This returns the index of the element that would be returned by a subsequent call to `next`

- `previous()`: This returns the previous element in the iteration and moves the cursor position backward
- `previousIndex()`: This returns the index of the element that would be returned by a subsequent call to `previous()`

There are some really useful extension functions, such as the following:

- `.asSequence()`: This creates a sequence that returns all elements from this iterator. The sequence is constrained to be iterated only once.
- `.forEach(operation: (T) -> Unit)`: This performs the given operation on each element of this iterator.
- `.iterator()`: This returns the given iterator itself and allows you to use an instance of the iterator in a for the loop.
- `.withIndex(): Iterator<IndexedValue<T>>`: This returns an iterator and wraps each value produced by this iterator with the `IndexedValue`, containing a value, and its index.

We have used `forEachIndexed`; this gives the extracted value at the index and the index itself. Check out the way we have iterated the user list:

```
fun showOnlineUsers(data: Json) {
  val onlineUsersList = document.getElementById("onlineUsersList")
  onlineUsersList?.let {
    val usersList = data["usersList"] as? Array<String>
    usersList?.forEachIndexed { index, nickName ->
     it.appendChild(getUserListItem(nickName))
    }
  }
}
```

Sending and receiving a message

Now, here comes the interesting part: sending and receiving a chat message. The flow is very simple: The client will emit the `new_message` event, which will be consumed by the server, and the server will emit it in the form of a broadcast for other clients. When the user clicks on **Send Message**, the `onSendMessageClicked` method will be called. It sends the value back to the view using `callback` and logs the message in the chat window. After successfully sending a message, it clears the input field as well.

Take a look at the following piece of code:

```kotlin
private fun onSendMessageClicked(): (Event) -> Unit {
  return {
    if (chatMessage?.isNotBlank() as Boolean) {
      val formContainer = document.getElementById("chatInputBox")
       as HTMLInputElement
      callback(chatMessage!!)
      logMessageFromMe(nickName = nickName, message =
       chatMessage!!)
      formContainer.value = ""
    }
  }
}
```

Null safety

We have defined `chatMessage` as nullable. Check out the declaration here:

```kotlin
private var chatMessage: String? = null
```

Kotlin is, by default, null safe. This means that, in Kotlin, objects cannot be null. So, if you want any object that can be null, you need to explicitly states that it can be nullable. With the safe call operator `?.`, we can write `if(obj !=null)` in the easiest way ever. The `if (chatMessage?.isNotBlank() == true)` can only be true if it's not null, and does not contain any whitespace. We do know how to use the `Elvis` operator while dealing with null. With the help of the `Elvis` operator, we can provide an alternative value if the object is null. We have used this feature in our code in a number of places. The following are some of the code snippets that highlight the usage of the safe call operator.

Removing the view if not null:

```kotlin
formContainer?.remove()
```

Iterating over list if not null:

```kotlin
usersList?.forEachIndexed { _, nickName ->
 it.appendChild(getUserListItem(nickName))
}
```

Appending a child if the `div` tag is not null:

```kotlin
onlineUsersList?.appendChild(getUserListItem
 (data["nickName"].toString()))
```

Getting a list of all child nodes if the `<ul>` tag is not null:

```
onlineUsersList?.childNodes
```

Checking whether the string is not null and not blank:

```
chatMessage?.isNotBlank()
```

Force unwraps

Sometimes, you will have to face a situation where you will be sure that the object will not be null at the time of accessing it. However, since you have declared nullable at the beginning, you will have to end up using force unwraps. Force unwraps have the syntax of `!!`. This means you have to fetch the value of the calling object, irrespective of it being nullable. We are explicitly reading the `chatMessage` value to pass its value in the `callback`. The following is the code:

```
callback(chatMessage!!)
```

 Force unwraps are something we should avoid. We should only use them while dealing with interoperability issues. Otherwise, using them is basically nothing but throwing away Kotlin's beautiful features.

Using the let function

With the help of Lambda and extension functions, Kotlin is providing yet another powerful feature in the form of let functions. The `let()` function helps you execute a series of steps on the calling object. This is highly useful when you want to perform some code where the calling object is used multiple times and you want to avoid a null check every time.

In the following code block, the `forEach` loop will only get executed if `onlineUsersList` is not null. We can refer to the calling object inside the `let` function using `it`:

```kotlin
fun showOnlineUsers(data: Json) {
  val onlineUsersList = document.getElementById("onlineUsersList")
  onlineUsersList?.let {
    val usersList = data["usersList"] as? Array<String>
    usersList?.forEachIndexed { _, nickName ->
     it.appendChild(getUserListItem(nickName))
    }
  }
}
```

Named parameter

What if we told you that while calling, it's not mandatory to pass the parameter in the same sequence that is defined in the function signature? Believe us. With Kotlin's named parameter feature, it's no longer a constraint. Take a look at the following function that has a `nickName` parameter and the second parameter is `message`:

```kotlin
private fun logMessageFromMe(nickName: String, message: String) {
    val onlineUsersList = document.getElementById("chatMessages")
    val li = document.create.li {
      div(classes = "sentMessages") {
        span(classes = "chatMessage") {
          +message
        }
        span(classes = "filledInitialsMe") {
          +getInitials(nickName)
        }
      }
    }
    onlineUsersList?.appendChild(li)
}
```

If you call a function such as `logMessageForMe(mrssage, nickName)`, it will be a blunder. However, with Kotlin, you can call a function without worrying about the sequence of the parameter. The following is the code for this:

```kotlin
fun showNewMessage(data: Json) {
    logMessage(message = data["message"] as String, nickName =
    data["nickName"] as String)
}
```

Note how the `showNewMessage()` function is calling it, passing `message` as the first parameter and `nickName` as the second parameter.

Disconnecting a socket

Whenever any user leaves the chat room, we will show other online users a message saying `x user left`. `Socket.IO` will send a notification to the server when any client disconnects. Upon receiving the disconnect, the event server will remove the user from the list, decrement the count of online users, and broadcast the event to all clients. The code can look something like this:

```kotlin
socket.on("disconnect", {
    usersList.remove(socket.nicknameas String)
    numOfUsers = numOfUsers.dec()
```

```
val userJoinedData = json(Pair("numOfUsers", numOfUsers),
  Pair("nickName", socket.nickname))
socket.broadcast.emit("user_left", userJoinedData)
})
```

Now, it's the client's responsibility to show the message for that event on the UI. The client will listen to the event and the `showUsersLeft` function will be called from the `ChatWindow` class.

The following code is used for receiving the `user_left` broadcast:

```
socket.on("user_left", { data ->
  chatWindow.showUserLeft(data)
})
```

The following displays the message with the nickname of the user who left the chat and the count of the remaining online users:

```
fun showUserLeft(data: Json) {
  logListItem("${data["nickName"]} left")
  logListItem(getParticipantsMessage(data["numOfUsers"] as Int))
}
```

Styling the page using CSS

We saw how to build a chat application using Kotlin, but without showing the data on a beautiful UI, the user will not like the web app. We have used some simple CSS to give a rich look to the `index.ejs` page. The styling code is kept inside `webapp/css/styles.css`.

However, we have done everything so far entirely and exclusively in Kotlin. So, it's better we apply CSS using Kotlin as well. You may have already observed that there are a few mentions of classes. It's nothing but applying the CSS in a Kotlin way. Take a look at how we have applied the classes while making HTML tree elements using a DSL:

```
fun showLogin() {
  val formContainer = document.getElementById("container") as
    HTMLDivElement
  val loginDiv = document.create.div {
    id = "loginDiv"
    h3(classes = "title") {
      +"Welcome to Kotlin Blueprints chat app"
    }
    input(classes = "nickNameInput") {
      id = "nickName"
```

```
              onInputFunction = onInput()
              maxLength = 16.toString()
              placeholder = "Enter your nick name"
          }
          button(classes = "loginButton") {
              +"Login"
              onClickFunction = onLoginButtonClicked()
          }
      }
  formContainer.appendChild(loginDiv)
  }
```

Summary

With this, we are coming to the end of another rollercoaster ride with Kotlin. It's time to believe now that you did it. You developed an entire chat application using Kotlin.

Kotlin code has the ability to transpile its code into JavaScript to run on the browser side and also into Node.js to run on the server side. You learned many exciting features of the Kotlin language. Kotlin, with Node.js, is very futuristic. It is definitely made for the long haul.

With its support for all the platforms, one can really be a full stack developer, and build the backend of applications, browser pages, and mobile apps for both Android and iOS. Isn't this great?

Kotlin is a nice, simple, and concise language. With Kotlin, you get the features of a wonderful JVM ecosystem, and, in most cases, JVM can easily outperform Node.js.

In the next chapter, we will take you on a ride where you will build a REST API using Kotlin.

6
News Feed – REST API

In the previous chapter, we saw how to develop web applications with the Spring Boot framework and expose the endpoints using **REST (representational state transfer)** APIs, although traditional web technologies can be utilized for providing REST web services, REST has become the de facto standard for communicating, and specialized REST frameworks are relevant in the world where servers would expose *only REST APIs*, but no user interface. In this chapter, we will cover web frameworks to build RESTful web services made with Kotlin in mind. These web frameworks will help you bootstrap your web applications in Kotlin. We will give an overview of all the web frameworks in Kotlin and build our news feed application using the Ktor web framework by JetBrains.

In this chapter, we will build our news feed application as RESTful web services with the Ktor framework made by JetBrains. You'll learn the following things:

- What is REST and a RESTful web service?
- Building web apps with Ktor
- Testing web services with Postman

What is REST?

REST stands for representational state transfer, which is a way for computers to communicate and interoperate with each other. It has become the de facto architectural style for web applications and the fact that it's built on top of the **hypertext transfer protocol (HTTP)** makes it more powerful. HTTP is as widespread as the internet itself, and REST services can reuse the same infrastructure, without needing to open any special ports in the firewall. Besides, one can leverage HTTP methods such as `GET`, `POST`, `PUT`, and so on to assign semantic meanings to the various operations on the server.

REST is extremely light weight and can be consumed/accessed by embedded devices or mobile devices where the computational power is low, and battery life is of high importance. This is because REST itself does not have any baggage on its own, as it relies heavily on the underlying HTTP machinery. Today HTTP/2 is spreading fast as a replacement for HTTP/1.1. With that, even the underlying HTTP protocol is getting lighter and faster; and this automatically benefits the REST servers.

JSON (JavaScript Object Notation) is the widely used format for the body of requests and responses in a RESTful service. But one can use other formats, such as XML, YML, or even define one's own format.

REST is stateless, which means no client data is stored on the server between requests. Due to this REST systems have fast performance, reliability, and the ability to grow by reusing components without affecting a system when it is managed or updated as a whole, even while it is running. Only the session state is stored on the client (that is, a browser or any other device supporting HTTP).

Let's say you have a URL:

GET https://newsapi.org/v1/article/1 and, when you send a request to this URL, it returns a response in JSON (which can be customized depending upon requirement). Consider the following code snippet:

```
{
    "author": "Kotlin Bot",
    "title": "Kotlin Census 2017",
    "description": "Every year we run the Kotlin Census survey so we
      can get the latest feedback from you, and how you are using
      Kotlin in your projects.",
    "url": "https://thenextweb.com/artificial-
      intelligence/2017/10/20/dna-techniques-could-transform-facial-
      recognition-technology/",
    "publishedAt": "2017-10-18T20:58:17Z"
}
```

What is Ktor?

The Ktor (http://ktor.io/) Framework is an open source web framework for quickly building web applications in Kotlin with minimal effort and without needing to set up technology constraints such as dependency injection, logging, and so on. It is made by JetBrains and is still in alpha. It will be stable in upcoming months.

The Kotlin website contains a list of all the web frameworks and to build RESTful web services. It is available at `https://kotlin.link/`. You can refer to the website and check out other frameworks.

Why Ktor?

Ktor is officially supported by JetBrains, which is one of the reasons to consider going with Ktor when developing web applications in Kotlin. Apart from that, Ktor has three key principles, which make it the framework of choice when building web applications in Kotlin.

Understanding unopinionated applications

The Ktor framework ships with very few setting-up constraints, such as logging, templating, messaging, persistence, serializing, dependency injection, and so on, for projects.

The features are installed into an application using a unified interception mechanism, which allows for the building of arbitrary pipelines. Thanks to this, it can be hosted in any servlet container with Servlet 3.0+ API support such as Tomcat, or as a standalone using Netty or Jetty.

The application's composition is unopinionated, which means it's entirely the developer's choice whether to use dependency injection framework or to do it manually; or to use functions or classes.

Asynchronous nature

Ktor uses Kotlin coroutines APIs with the help of pipeline machinery. It provides easy-to-use asynchronous programming models and all the hosts are implemented using an asynchronous I/O to avoid thread blocking.

Highly testable

The Ktor framework was designed with testing in mind, that's why it comes with a special test environment, which emulates web servers to some extent, without actually doing any networking, by hooking it directly into internal machinery, which processes `ApplicationCall` directly. Hence, there is less need for mocking and, due to this, the performance of application calls is faster.

In a nutshell, it's perfectly capable of testing application logic, but you should make sure to set up integration tests with a real embedded web server.

Deploying the Ktor app

The Ktor application runs in an embedded web server. It supports deployments in many environments, such as Netty, Jetty, and web servers such as Tomcat. For other hosts, refer to this link: `http://ktor.io/artifacts.html` for a list of available modules.

Let's build our news application

We are going to build a news feed application to understand how to build a web application using Ktor and Kotlin. You will learn how to use Ktor and Kotlin to build a robust and testable web application quickly with minimal effort or constraints, while also having fun with Kotlin's features.

The idea is to build a RESTful news feed application that will show a list of the latest news from various sources such as Google News. It doesn't generate the news itself. It fetches the news from various news sources.

News provider

We will be using News API from `https://newsapi.org/` to fetch the latest news from various sources. It is a simple, free, and easy-to-use API that returns JSON from over 70 different sources. It is recommended to get an API key from News API because we will require it in our application later to fetch the news.

There are two APIs provided by the news provider—one to fetch news sources, and a second to fetch news articles.

Fetching news sources

This provides a list of the news sources and blogs available on News API:

```
GET https://newsapi.org/v1/sources
```

Fetching news articles

This provides a list of live articles from a news source or blog:

```
GET https://newsapi.org/v1/articles
```

The following are the parameters that are required for fetching news articles:

source	(required): The identifier for the news source or blog you want headlines from. Use the `/sources` endpoint to locate this or use the sources index (`https://newsapi.org/sources`).
apiKey	(required): Your API key. Alternatively, you can provide this via the `X-Api-Key` HTTP header.

Preview

As we are building a RESTful web service, we won't be having any particular UI for the application.

Features

The features in this application are technically endpoints providing the following:

- A list of all the supported news sources
- A list of news articles from a particular news source

The following diagram represents the features in this application:

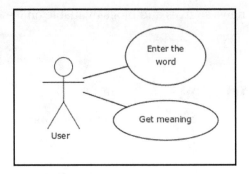

Architecture

We only have Ktor running on the backend and REST APIs to consume the functionality provided by the backend:

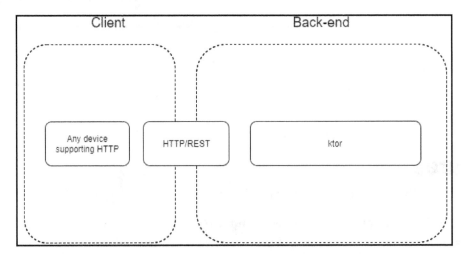

Setting up the IDE

Let's create the project in an **integrated development environment** (**IDE**) of our choice. I'm using IntelliJ Community Edition to build the application. You can use any other IDE such as Eclipse, or download IntelliJ Community Edition from the following link: `https://www.jetbrains.com/idea/download/`.

Prerequisites

The following are the prerequisites before you start the project:

- The most recent version of IntelliJ IDEA Community Edition
- Kotlin and Gradle plugins enabled (they should be, by default)

Creating the project

Create a new project in IntelliJ and select **Gradle.** Then select **Java** and Kotlin as they are mentioned as follows:

1. Open IntelliJ.
2. Click **File | New | Project**.
3. Select **Gradle** with **Java** and Kotlin.
4. Enter the Group ID: `com.news` (you can change it).
   Enter the **Artifact Id**: NewsFeed (you can change it).

5. Check the optional checkboxes for **Use auto-import** and **Create separate module per source set**, as shown in the following screenshot:

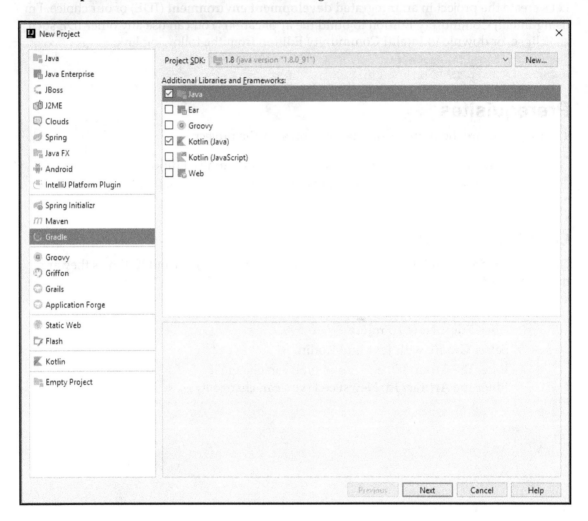

Project structure

The project structure is divided into two modules:

- `main`: This contains the development code
- `test`: This contains tests for the application

The main module contains:

- `kotlin` directory (similar to Java) where all the Kotlin is placed
- `resources` directory contains static resources, such as HTML, CSS, JS, and images for the web application

 It is not required that the Kotlin code goes into the `kotlin` directory, but it is a good convention to follow. If you place it under some other directory, then make sure to make appropriate changes to `build.gradle`.

Here is the package structure with the base package as `com.news` that we follow. Feel free to follow a similar structure in your projects:

- `routes`: This contains all of the URL routing logic

The following screenshot represents the project explorer:

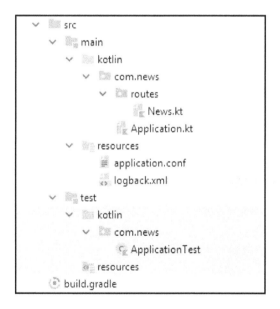

Deploying

To run the application you need to set the `main` class as one of the following in your IDE:

- Netty: use `io.ktor.netty.DevelopmentHost`
- Jetty: use `io.ktor.jetty.DevelopmentHost`

Deploying in IntelliJ IDEA

The following are those steps involved in using IntelliJ IDEA for deploying an application:

1. Create a new run configuration using `Application` as a template
2. For the main class use one of the following hosts:
    - Netty: Use `io.ktor.netty.DevelopmentHost`
    - Jetty: Use `io.ktor.jetty.DevelopmentHost`
3. Specify the module to be used
4. Save the configuration with a name
5. Hit run and go to `localhost:8080` in your browser

Setting up the build script

We will be using the Gradle build system for our project.

Adding Kotlin dependency

Kotlin language is added as a Gradle dependency in the project:

```
// Kotlin
compile "org.jetbrains.kotlin:kotlin-stdlib-jre8:$kotlin_version"
```

Adding Ktor dependencies

The `Ktor` file is located on `bintray` and it has a dependency on the coroutines library available in `kotlinx`, so we will need to add the following repositories to the repositories block:

```
maven { url "http://dl.bintray.com/kotlin/ktor" }
maven { url "https://dl.bintray.com/kotlin/kotlinx" }
```

We will add an extra property for holding the value of the latest version of Ktor:

```
ext.ktor_version = '0.9.0-alpha1'
```

Now add the `ktor-core` dependency in our `build.gradle`:

```
// ktor
compile "io.ktor:ktor:$ktor_version"
```

As we discussed earlier, Ktor can be deployed in various environments. For our news feed application, we will use Netty as our server by adding an extra dependency:

```
compile "io.ktor:ktor-server-netty:$ktor_version"
```

Coroutines are still an experimental feature in Kotlin, hence we will need to tell the compiler that it's OK to use them to avoid warnings:

```
kotlin {
  experimental {
    coroutines "enable"
  }
}
```

 It's a good practice to maintain versions in Gradle using extra properties such as `ext.ktor_version`. It helps in making more readable, maintainable, and easy-to-upgrade versions of your dependencies.

Configuring logging

Ktor uses SLF4J (`https://www.slf4j.org/`) for logging by default. The following message is shown on running the application, if you don't add a logging provider:

```
SLF4J: Failed to load class "org.slf4j.impl.StaticLoggerBinder".
SLF4J: Defaulting to no-operation (NOP) logger implementation
SLF4J: See http://www.slf4j.org/codes.html#StaticLoggerBinder for further
details.
```

We can set up the logging provider to understand what is happening with the app by adding an additional Gradle dependency:

```
compile "ch.qos.logback:logback-classic:1.2.3"
```

Now, at least, we get good levels of logging information. But let's tweak them so they are more useful, in order to do that, we need to create a configuration file named `logback.xml` in the `main/resources` directory with the following content:

```xml
<configuration>
  <appender name="STDOUT"
   class="ch.qos.logback.core.ConsoleAppender">
    <encoder>
      <pattern>%d{YYYY-MM-dd HH:mm:ss.SSS} [%thread] %-5level
        %logger{36} - %msg%n</pattern>
    </encoder>
  </appender>

  <root level="trace">
    <appender-ref ref="STDOUT"/>
  </root>

  <logger name="org.eclipse.jetty" level="INFO"/>
  <logger name="io.netty" level="INFO"/>

</configuration>
```

With this, we get sensible and useful logs such as:

```
- Application - Application started:
 io.ktor.application.Application@333d4a8c
- Application - 200 OK: GET - /
```

Adding Fuel

Our news feeder fetches the news from an external REST endpoint. To fetch it, we require an HTTP client but, unfortunately, Ktor doesn't come with its own HTTP client. Luckily we are in Kotlin world, hence we can use any Java library, and that's why we will be using the Fuel (`https://github.com/kittinunf/Fuel`) library as our HTTP client.

It's not absolutely necessary to go with the Fuel library. You can choose from a plethora of networking libraries that are available for Java. Fuel is extremely easy to add and use.

What is Fuel?

Fuel is an extremely simple networking library for Kotlin/Java and Android. It has tons of features, from basic support for HTTP requests, such as GET and POST, to RxJava. It even supports requests of an asynchronous nature, which is a bonus.

 To find out more about Fuel, visit `https://github.com/kittinunf/Fuel`.

Adding Gradle dependency

We add Fuel dependency in our `build.gradle` file:

```
compile 'com.github.kittinunf.fuel:fuel:1.11.0'
```

Quick sample

Let's look at a quick sample using Fuel. The sample is quite similar to what we are going to use later in our news feed app.

The Fuel library supports two types of request—Async and blocking.

Asynchronous mode

In asynchronous mode, the thread is not blocked until completion. It doesn't wait for a response, instead a callback is called when the response is returned, as shown in the following code snippet:

```
"https://newsapi.org/".httpGet().responseString { request,
  response, result ->
    //do something with response
    when (result) {
      is Result.Failure -> {
        error = result.getAs()
      }
      is Result.Success -> {
        data = result.getAs()
      }
    }
}
```

In the preceding example, we send a GET request to the URL and received the response as a callback with success or failure flags.

Blocking mode

Unlike in asynchronous mode, in blocking mode the thread is blocked until the response is returned from the URL. It has exact parameters and features that are similar to asynchronous mode, except for the callback:

```
val (request, response, result) =
  "https://newsapi.org/".httpGet().responseString()
```

Completing Gradle script

After adding all the dependencies, the build.gradle file should look something like this:

```
group 'com.news'
version '1.0-SNAPSHOT'

buildscript {
  ext.kotlin_version = '1.1.51'
  ext.ktor_version = '0.9.0-alpha-2'
  ext.log_version = '1.2.3'
  ext.fuel_version = '1.11.0'

  repositories {
    mavenCentral()
  }
  dependencies {
    classpath "org.jetbrains.kotlin:kotlin-gradle-
      plugin:$kotlin_version"
  }
}

apply plugin: 'java'
apply plugin: 'kotlin'

sourceCompatibility = 1.8

repositories {
  mavenCentral()
  maven { url "https://dl.bintray.com/kotlin/kotlinx" }
  maven { url "https://dl.bintray.com/kotlin/ktor" }
}
```

```
dependencies {
  //Kotlin
  compile "org.jetbrains.kotlin:kotlin-stdlib-jre8:$kotlin_version"

  // Ktor
  compile "io.ktor:ktor:$ktor_version"
  compile "io.ktor:ktor-server-netty:$ktor_version"

  // Logging
  compile "ch.qos.logback:logback-classic:$log_version"

  // Fuel
  compile "com.github.kittinunf.fuel:fuel:$fuel_version"

  testCompile group: 'junit', name: 'junit', version: '4.12'
}

kotlin {
  experimental {
    coroutines "enable"
  }
}

compileKotlin {
  kotlinOptions.jvmTarget = "1.8"
}
compileTestKotlin {
  kotlinOptions.jvmTarget = "1.8"
}
```

Let's code!

Our project is ready with the required project structure, and Gradle dependency and configuration. Now it's time to write the application code.

Application configuration

In Ktor, there are two ways to configure the application parameters:

- From Kotlin code
- Using configuration files

It's recommended to use a configuration file, because with configuration files, if you change any of the parameters later, then you won't need to recompile the code in future as there is no change in the Kotlin code. You'll only need to restart the application on the server.

Hence, we create a configuration file named `application.conf` in the `main/resources` directory of our project with the following content:

```
ktor {
  deployment {
    port = 8080
  }

  application {
    modules = [ com.news.ApplicationKt.main ]
  }
}
```

Deployment block

The deployment block contains configuration, such as port numbers, auto-reload, and so on.

Application block

The application block is an important block that points to our application main (Kotlin code), which we will be looking into in the next section.

Application main

An application instance is the *main* unit of a Ktor application. It is the starting point of our application. A request (which can be an HTTP, HTTP/2, or Socket request) comes in the application and is converted to an `ApplicationCall`. It then goes through a pipeline that contains one or more previously installed interceptors; these provide certain functionalities such as routing, compression, and many more.

The `ApplicationCall` provides access to two main properties:

- `ApplicationRequest`: This corresponds to the incoming request
- `ApplicationResponse`: This corresponds to the outgoing response

It also provides some useful functions to help respond to client requests.

Let's look at our main `Application.kt` file:

```
/**
 * Starting point
 */
fun Application.main() {
  install(DefaultHeaders)
  // Adds logging
  install(CallLogging)
  // Adds URL routes
  install(Routing) {
    get("/") {
      call.respondText("Hello readers!", ContentType.Text.Html)
    }
    newsSources()
    newsArticles()
  }
}
```

We have an extension function `main()` on the `Application` class, instead of our typical `main()` function. We have mentioned this function as our starting point in the `application.conf`, which we saw previously.

We perform our application setup in this function, setting up the logs, URL routes, and so on, by using `install()` from the Ktor package. The `install()` function sets up the required features for the application.

Installing routing

The most important feature is routing, in which we specify the URLs that the application is going to handle. It is a feature that is installed into an application to simplify and structure page requests handling. There are a couple of ways to specify the URLs.

The `get`, `post`, `put`, `delete`, `head`, and `options` functions are convenient shortcuts for a flexible and powerful routing system to specify any HTTP method such as GET and POST.

It is built in a DSL manner.

Simple routing

It is the easiest way to add all the URLs and their corresponding functions. The only catch is that there is no separation of concern, which means that the code is not self-dependent and not modular either.

Example:

```
get("/") {
    call.respondText("Hello readers!", ContentType.Text.Html)
}
```

In this case, the URL pattern and its action (function) are specified in the application file.

Modular routing

With modular routing, we separate the URL handling logic into different files for easier maintenance and to achieve a separation of concern.

For example:

```
install(Routing) {
    newsSources()
    newsArticles()
}
```

In this case, we just specify the list of functions to handle the routing, while the actual routing logic is defined in a different location or file.

We are adding these routes to our `Routing` module. Hence we need to create extension functions on the `Route` class to understand that it contains URL mapping (routing).

Understanding route paths

Sometimes building a routing tree by hand can be very inconvenient. Hence, there is the path, which is a parameter to the route function, that is processed to build routing trees. First, it is split into path segments by the / delimiter. Each segment generates a nested routing node. These two variants are equivalent:

```
// Variant 1
route("/foo/bar") { ... }

// Variant 2
route("/foo") {
    route("bar") { ... }
}
```

Path parameters

The path can also contain parameters that match specific path segments and capture its value into parameters properties of an application call:

```
get("/user/{id}") {
  val id = call.parameters["id"]
}
```

Let's look at the newsSources function:

```
/**
 * Get list of all news sources
 */
fun Route.newsSources() {
  get("/news-source") {
    val (_, _, result) =
      "https://newsapi.org/v1/sources".httpGet().responseString()
    call.respondText(result.get(), ContentType.Application.Json)
  }
}
```

The function contains a GET request specified using the get function from Route. Inside the get function, we get call, which is an instance of ApplicationCall to handle requests and responses.

We send a GET request to the News API, fetch all the news sources or blogs, and return the data as JSON.

For its usage:

GET http://localhost:8080/news-source

The response will be somewhat like this:

```
{
  "status": "ok",
  "sources": [
  {
    "id": "abc-news-au",
    "name": "ABC News (AU)",
    "description": "Australia's most trusted source of local,
      national and world news. Comprehensive, independent, in-depth
      analysis, the latest business, sport, weather and more.",
    "url": "http://www.abc.net.au/news",
    "category": "general",
    "language": "en",
    "country": "au",
```

```
        "urlsToLogos": {
          "small": "",
          "medium": "",
          "large": ""
        },
        "sortBysAvailable": [
          "top"
        ]
      },
      // Other sources
      ...
      ]
    }
```

Let's look at the `newsArticles` function:

```
/**
 * Get news from a particular source
 */
fun Route.newsArticles() {
  get("/news/{source}") {
    val source = call.parameters["source"]
    val (_, _, result) = "https://newsapi.org/v1/articles?
    source=$source".httpGet()
    .header("x-api-key" to "YOUR_NEWS_API_KEY")
    .responseString()
    call.respondText(result.get(), ContentType.Application.Json)
  }
}
```

The function contains a GET request specified using the `get` function from `Route` with a path parameter as the `source` and handler, which means the logic is to trigger when the URL is hit. Inside the `get` function, we get `call`, which is an instance of `ApplicationCall` to handle requests and responses and the value of the path parameter `source`.

We send a GET request to the News API with the news source value from the path parameter, and an API key got from `https://newsapi.org/`. This API key is sent with the header with the key `x-api-key`, and we get top news articles from specified news sources or blogs in JSON format.

For its usage:

```
GET http://localhost:8080/news/techcrunch
```

The response will be somewhat like this:

```
{
  "status": "ok",
  "source": "techcrunch",
  "sortBy": "top",
  "articles": [
    {
      "author": "Lucas Matney",
      "title": "Google introduces Neural Networks API in developer
      preview of Android 8.1",
      "description": "Google is starting to seed to devs a new
      developer beta (8.1) of Android Oreo. The big highlight here
      is the new Neural Networks API, which brings..",
      "url": "https://techcrunch.com/2017/10/25/google-introduces-
      neural-networks-api-in-developer-preview-of-android-8-1/",
      "urlToImage":
      "https://tctechcrunch2011.files.wordpress.com/2017/08/oreo-
      android-multiple.png",
      "publishedAt": "2017-10-25T21:36:58Z"
    },
    // More news articles....
  ]
}
```

We have our application ready to run and test!

Testing

Our news feed application is ready, but it's not production ready until it is tested.

Adding Gradle dependency

We need to add JUnit and Ktor dependencies in the `build.gradle` file to test the application:

```
// Testing
testCompile group: 'junit', name: 'junit', version: '4.12'
testCompile "io.ktor:ktor-server-test-host:$ktor_version"
```

Testing the application

We have three URL endpoints in our application, two of which return JSON data for which we will use an external tool named Postman to test them.

Testing the index URL

The preceding test case gets an instance of our application and sends a get request on the specified URL, which in this is /, aka an index URL, and it checks if the status is OK - 200 and content is `Hello readers!`:

```
class ApplicationTest {
  @Test
  fun `check index page`() = withTestApplication(Application::main)
  {
    with(handleRequest(HttpMethod.Get, "/")) {
      assertEquals(HttpStatusCode.OK, response.status())
      assertEquals("Hello readers!", response.content)
    }
  }
}
```

Testing JSON using Postman

We use the Postman tool to verify if our URLs are returning expected JSON data. Postman is an extremely simple tool. Just enter the URL, select the HTTP request type and send the request, and wait for the response from the server.

Testing news sources using Postman

Let's test the news sources API by fetching all the news sources using Postman:

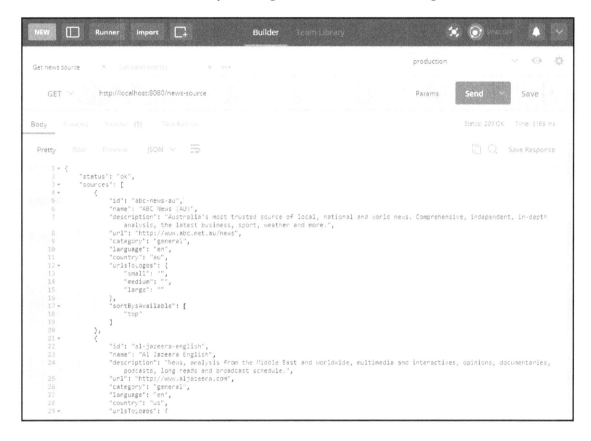

Testing news sources using Postman

Let's test the news articles API by fetching news articles using Postman:

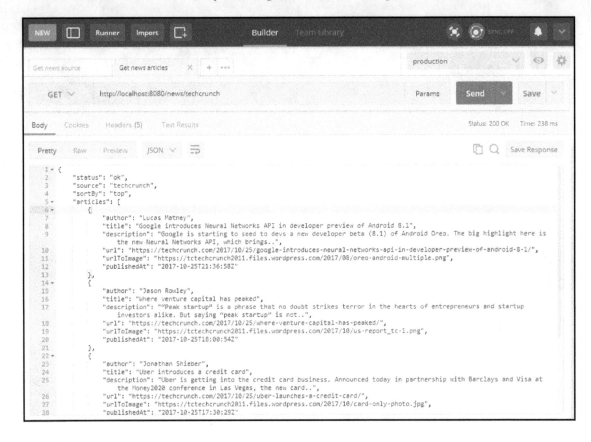

Summary

Ktor enables quick development with less hassle from technological constraints, such as setting up logging, templates, dependency injection, and so on. The application code is especially concise, thanks to Kotlin's nature, which adds to its readability.

The downside with Ktor is its lack of documentation and community, which means it's difficult to start and, if you face some issues with it, then it's even more difficult because of the smaller community that exists to help resolve them. Moreover, the framework has not reached v1.0 at the time of writing. It should reach v1.0 pretty soon, though. Overall it's a great framework for building web applications instantly and completely with Kotlin.

We have successfully built our production-ready news feed application as a RESTful web service, which can be used to read the latest news with the Ktor framework while leveraging amazing features such as DSL, co-routines of Kotlin. We also saw how to write test cases in Kotlin, which are a great way to start writing Kotlin code, in case you're afraid of writing actual logic, and test our service using the Postman tool.

In the next chapter, we will look at how to build applications using Kotlin/Native to run applications without a **virtual machine** (**VM**) such as iOS or embedded systems.

7

CSV Reader in Kotlin Native

In all the previous chapters, we either used Kotlin on JVM or Kotlin on JS to run our Kotlin code. In this chapter, we will look at Kotlin Native, which is Kotlin without a **VM** (**Virtual Machine**) and is supposedly the future of Kotlin, and how to build multiplatform projects. At the end of the chapter, we will create a command-line based CSV reader that prints the unique entries of the column and their count from the specified CSV file (dataset).

In this chapter, you'll learn the following things:

- What is Kotlin Native?
- Installing Kotlin Native
- Building apps with Kotlin Native
- What is multiplatform Kotlin?

What is Kotlin Native?

Kotlin Native is an LLVM backend for the Kotlin compiler that is designed to run on areas without a VM. It uses an LLVM toolchain to generate the runtime implementation and native code.

It is primarily designed to allow compilation for platforms where virtual machines are not desirable or possible (such as iOS and embedded systems), or where we need to produce a self-contained program that does not require additional runtime.

It fully supports interoperability within the native code, that is, C language code. It works similarly to how Kotlin/JVM interoperates with Java language code. For platform libraries, the corresponding interoperating libraries are available out of the box, while for other libraries, there is a tool (`https://github.com/JetBrains/kotlin-native/blob/master/INTEROP.md`) to generate an interoperating library from a C header file, with full support for all C language features. It also supports interoperability with Objective/C code for macOS and iOS.

IDE support for Kotlin Native is available in the form of plugins for CLion at `https://www.jetbrains.com/clion/` (IDE for C/C++ language by JetBrains), which supports CMake as the build system.

The advantages of Kotlin Native include the following:

- It runs without a VM
- It compiles down native machine code
- It has the ability to produce a self-contained executable
- It is cross-platform (all supported platforms are listed in the following *Target platforms* section)
- It offers interoperability with C code

The compiler is open source and is available under the Apache 2 OSS license.

 Kotlin Native is still in its early stages and is currently in the development phase. The latest preview release is currently v0.4.

Target platforms

Kotlin Native currently supports the following platforms:

- Windows (x86_64 only, at the moment)
- Linux (x86_64, arm32, MIPS, and MIPS little endian)
- MacOS (x86_64)
- iOS (arm64 only)
- Android (arm32 and arm64)
- WebAssembly (wasm32 only)

We are using the Windows platform, in this chapter, to build and execute the program. You can use whichever platform you are comfortable with.

Multiplatform Kotlin

Along with all the advantages of Kotlin Native mentioned in the previous sections, what makes it so special is its ability to share code across platforms. This enables the reuse of code, and there will, therefore, be a single language. This is called a multiplatform Kotlin; we will be discussing it in detail in the next section.

The following diagram illustrates how Kotlin can be used on various platforms:

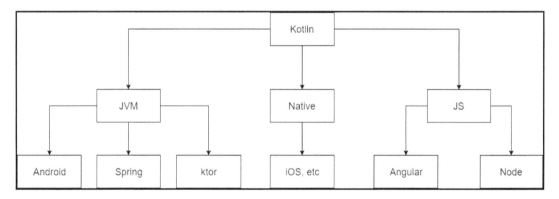

Installing Kotlin Native

We can install Kotlin Native from the source, or grab the binaries from the web. Feel free to go with any method you prefer; the end result will be the same.

Installing from the source

In order to install Kotlin Native on our machine, we need to compile it from the source. Follow these steps to download the source and compile it:

1. Clone the Kotlin Native compiler source using the following command:

```
git clone https://github.com/JetBrains/kotlin-native.git
```

2. Let's switch to the cloned directory using `cd kotlin-native`.
3. Download the dependencies using `./gradlew dependencies:update`.
4. Then build the compiler and libraries. We should use `./gradlew bundle`, but it can take a few hours to build. Therefore, we will build only with the host compiler and the libraries using `./gradlew dist distPlatformLibs`, which should build pretty quickly.
5. Add the Kotlin compiler to the environment variables (the steps to add it vary). The following command should ideally work on most systems:`export PATH=./dist/bin:$PATH`. For Windows, perform the following steps:
    1. Open **Edit the system environment variables.**
    2. Select **Environment Variables.**
    3. Click on **PATH variable**.
    4. Add the path of the `kotlin-native` bin directory (Windows example: `J:\Work\kotlin-native\dist\bin`).
    5. Save it!
6. Open the command prompt or terminal.
7. Run `kotlinc -version` to verify whether or not the Kotlin Native compiler installed successfully.

You need to have Git pre-installed on your machine to run the `git clone` command. If you don't have it, then you can install it from `https://git-scm.com/downloads`.

The following is the output received upon executing the `kotlinc -version` command:

```
C:\Windows\system32\cmd.exe

C:\Users\Akshay>kotlinc -version
info: kotlinc-native 1.2.0-rc-39 (JRE 1.8.0_91-b15)
error: you have not specified any compilation arguments. No output has been produced.

C:\Users\Akshay>
```

Kotlin Native uses Kotlin v1.2-RC because it supports multiple platforms and includes features for code-sharing.

Installing from binaries

You can grab the binaries directly depending on your platform, from the following links:

- For macOS: `http://download.jetbrains.com/kotlin/native/kotlin-native-macos-0.4.tar.gz`.
- For Linux: `http://download.jetbrains.com/kotlin/native/kotlin-native-linux-0.4.tar.gz`.
- For Windows: `http://download.jetbrains.com/kotlin/native/kotlin-native-windows-0.4.zip`.

After downloading, follow these steps:

1. Extract the ZIP or TAR.
2. Follow step 5 in the *Installing from the source* section.
3. Open the command prompt or terminal.
4. Run `kotlinc -version` to verify whether or not the Kotlin Native compiler installed successfully.

 Please note that the preceding download links are for Kotlin Native v0.4, which is the latest preview version at the moment.

Testing the installation

Let's test if the Kotlin compiler was compiled properly, and added to the environment variables, by running a simple *Hello World* program.

Here is a simple *Hello World* program. I'm pretty sure you will notice this in the following Kotlin code, but there is no difference in the language syntax or standard library functions, as shown in the following code snippet:

```
fun main(args: Array<String>) {
  println("Hello World!")
}
```

Save this program in a Kotlin file named `Hello.kt`.

To run the program, we use the `kotlinc` command, as follows:

```
kotlinc hello.kt -o hello
```

In the preceding code, `hello.kt` is the name of the file containing the Kotlin code and `-o` `hello` specifies the output filename.

For an optimized compilation, use the `-opt` flag:

```
kotlinc hello.kt -o hello -opt
```

Take a look at the following screenshot:

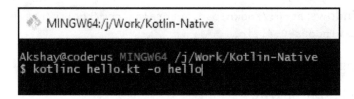

On successful compilation, you should see an executable file named `hello` or `hello.exe` on Windows.

Let's run the executable output using the following:

```
./hello
```

You should see the **Hello World!** output printed on the console:

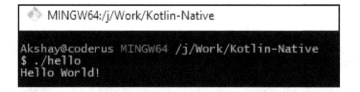

Memory management

Kotlin Native is designed potentially to enable different memory management solutions for different target platforms. That's because it doesn't ship with a VM, and machine code is not always faster than JVM-based bytecode, as JVM does some optimizations to the code on the fly.

For example, in the future, it may make sense to have a tracing GC for server/desktop platforms, while ARC makes a lot more sense on iOS. Some platforms may only need manual memory management and may get an even smaller Kotlin Native runtime in return.

The latest preview features *automatic reference counting* with a cycle collector on top, but what the final memory management solution(s) will look like is unknown at this point.

Building our app

We will be building a command-line based CSV reader that prints the unique entries of the columns and their counts, based on user input in Kotlin Native.

Writing the main function

Kotlin Native has the same language syntax and includes the standard library. Hence, the `main` function in Kotlin Native looks the same as the `main` function in JVM or JS. It is similar to the following syntax:

```
// Starting point
fun main(args: Array<String>) {
  // Rest of code over here..
}
```

The `main` function takes `args`, which contains the arguments from the command line.

Reading command-line arguments

We will be taking two arguments from the command line:

- The name of the CSV file to read
- The column number to find unique entries from

The following code block shows how to read arguments passed from the command line:

```
// Get command line input
if (args.size != 2) {
  println("Usage: csv_filename column_number")
  return
}
val fileName = args[0]
val columnNumber = args[1].toInt()
```

For example, `csv.exe books.csv 1`.

Opening the file

Opening the file with Kotlin/JVM is pretty easy because Java provides APIs to perform CRUD operations on a file. These APIs are not available because Kotlin Native is Kotlin without a VM. Hence, there are only the APIs provided by the standard library, which unfortunately doesn't provide APIs to play with a file.

This is where we are going to leverage Kotlin Native's feature to enable interoperability with the C code, and use its API to open the CSV file using the `fopen` function.

 Files can be closed, using the `fclose` function, by passing the stream (`FILE`), though all files opened are automatically closed upon normal program termination.

The `fopen` function opens the file whose name has been passed in the first parameter (filename) and returns a stream using the `FILE` (`http://www.cplusplus.com/reference/cstdio/FILE/`) pointer that can be used in future operations.

The second parameter (mode) defines which operations can be performed on the stream:

```
FILE * fopen (const char * filename, const char * mode);
```

The parameters that can be used are as follows:

- **Filename**: A string containing the name of the file.
- **Mode**: A string containing the file access mode. The following table shows an extensive list of access modes:

r	read: Open the file for input operations. Note that the file must exist.
w	write: Create an empty file for output operations. If a file with the same name already exists, its contents are discarded and the file is treated as a new empty file.
a	append: Open the file for output at the end of a file. Output operations always write data at the end of the file, expanding it. The file is created if it does not exist.
r+	read/update: Open a file for the update (both for input and output). The file must exist.
w+	write/update: Create an empty file and open it for the update (both for input and output). If a file with the same name already exists, its contents are discarded and the file is treated as a new, empty file.

`a+`	append/update: Open a file for the update (both for input and output), with all output operations writing data at the end of the file. Repositioning operations (fseek: `http://www.cplusplus.com/reference/cstdio/fseek/`, fsetpos: `http://www.cplusplus.com/reference/cstdio/fsetpos/`, and rewind: `http://www.cplusplus.com/reference/cstdio/rewind/`) affect the next input operations, but output operations move the position back to the end of the file. The file is created if it does not exist.

We open the CSV file (the filename is received from the command-line arguments) in reading mode. If the file stream is null, then we print an error, using `perror`, and exit the program, as shown in the following code:

```
// Open the file
val file = fopen(fileName, "r")
if (file == null) {
  perror("Failed to open the file named $fileName")
  return
}
```

The `perror` function prints a descriptive error message to `stderr`. First, the string passed by `str` is printed, followed by a colon and then a space:

```
void perror (const char * str);
```

Here, `str` is a string containing a custom message to print before the error message itself.

Reading the file contents

We are going to leverage C interoperability to read the contents of a CSV file using the `fgets` function.

The `fgets` function reads characters from the file stream and stores them as a C string until (num-1) characters have been read or either a newline or the **end-of-the-file** (EOF) is reached, whichever happens first. The function stops reading when a newline \n character is encountered, but it is considered a valid character and included in the string copied to `str`:

```
char * fgets (char * str, int num, FILE * stream);
```

The parameters are as follows:

- str: Pointer to str where the content read is stored
- num: Maximum number of characters to be copied into str
- stream: Pointer to the FILE stream that identifies an input stream

 fgets is different to the gets function and accepts a stream argument, but also allows you for the specification of the maximum size of str, and includes in the string any ending newline character.

To read the content, we need to create a pointer to store the file content (into a buffer), for which we need to allocate memory. There are currently several different ways to allocate memory. The easiest way in Kotlin Native is to use the NativePlacement interface along with a memScoped block, as represented in the following code snippet:

```
memScoped {
    val bufferLength = 64 * 1024
    // Allocating memory
    val buffer = allocArray<ByteVar>(bufferLength)
}
```

The memory allocation is scoped using the memScoped function. This is great because, once the scope of the function is left, any allocated memory will be eligible for the garbage collector.

Counting unique entries

We read each line of the file by continuously iterating the file stream until we reach the end of the stream with the help of the fgets function, and break the loop if we hit null, which indicates the end of the stream.

We need to find the unique entries from the specified column (column_number from the command line arguments) and increment the occurrence by checking if it already exists in the ;map with the key, that is, String and value, that is, Int, as shown in the following code snippet:

```
// Map
val result = mutableMapOf<String, Int>()

while (true) {
    // Get line
    val nextLine = fgets(buffer, bufferLength, file)?.toKString() ?:
```

```
    break

    // Split line
    val records = nextLine.split(",")
    val key = records[columnNumber]

    // Adjust the occurrence count
    val current = result[key] ?: 0
    result[key] = current + 1
}
```

Converting to Kotlin string

Unlike other pointers, the parameters of `const char*` type are represented as a Kotlin strings. So it is possible to pass any Kotlin string to the binding, expecting C string.

To manually convert a C string to a Kotlin string, use the following:

```
fun CPointer<ByteRef>.toKString(): String
```

This extension function helps to convert `const char*` to a Kotlin string.

Splitting strings

We need to split the line into a list of strings to get the values of columns into an index based list. Hence, we use an extension function named `split`, which is injected into `CharSequence`. It is part of the standard library.

The `split` function splits the specified string, using the specified deliminator, and returns a list of strings:

```
fun CharSequence.split(vararg delimiters: String, ignoreCase:
  Boolean, limit: Int) : List<String>
```

The following parameters can be used:

- `delimiters`: One or more deliminator to split the string.
- `ignoreCase`: True to ignore character case when matching a delimiter. By default it's false.
- `limit`: Maximum number of substrings to return. By default, it's zero, meaning that no limit is set.

Let's look at an example of the `split` function. The CSV file contains a line, as shown in the following pattern—the name of the book, the status of the book, and the publisher of the book:

```
Kotlin Blueprints,Coming soon,Packt
```

Using the `split` function and specifying a deliminator as a comma (`,`), it returns a list of strings:

```
["Kotlin Blueprints", "Coming soon", "Packt"]
```

Printing the result

Finally, we print the result by iterating the result map:

```
// Prints the result
result.forEach {
  println("${it.key} -> ${it.value}")
}
```

Complete code

Finally, after pooling all the bits and pieces of the code explained in the previous sections, here is the complete code:

```
import kotlinx.cinterop.*
import platform.posix.*

/**
 * The starting point
 */
fun main(args: Array<String>) {

  // Get command line input
  if (args.size != 2) {
    println("Usage: csv_filename column_number")
    return
  }
  val fileName = args[0]
  val columnNumber = args[1].toInt()

  // Open the file
  val file = fopen(fileName, "r")
  if (file == null) {
    perror("Failed to open the file named $fileName")
```

```kotlin
      return
    }

    val result = mutableMapOf<String, Int>()

    try {
      memScoped {
        // Memory allocation for buffer
        val bufferLength = 64 * 1024
        val buffer = allocArray<ByteVar>(bufferLength)

        while (true) {
          // Get line
          val nextLine = fgets(buffer, bufferLength,
            file)?.toKString() ?: break

          // Split line
          val records = nextLine.split(",")
          val key = records[columnNumber]

          // Adjust the occurance count
          val current = result[key] ?: 0
          result[key] = current + 1
        }
      }
    } finally {
      fclose(file)
    }

    // Prints the result
    result.forEach {
      println("${it.key} -> ${it.value}")
    }
}
```

Running the program

It's time to run our program. Before that, though, let's prepare our dataset to execute the program.

Understanding the dataset

The following table shows the contents of the CSV file (named `books.csv`) on which we are going to run the program. The structure is pretty simple, with just three columns—the name of the book, the status of the book, and the publisher of the book:

Name	Status	Publisher
Kotlin Blueprints	Coming soon	Packt
Reactive Programming in Kotlin	Published	Packt
Mastering Android Development with Kotlin	Published	Packt
Kotlin Programming by Example	Published	Packt
Python Programming Blueprints	Published	Packt

Compiling the program

The program is compiled using the following command:

```
kotlinc CSV.kt -o CSV
```

In the preceding code, `CSV.kt` is the name of the file containing the Kotlin code and `-o CSV` specifies the output filename.

On successful compilation, the command generates two new files, namely `CSV.exe` (Windows executable) and `CSV.kt.bc`:

Executing the program

The program is executed by executing the output file (`.exe` in Windows) and passing two command-line arguments, namely the CSV filename and column number.

The files are organized (in my case) as shown in the following screenshot:

books.csv	20/11/2017 12:02	CSV File	1 KB
CSV.exe	20/11/2017 11:47	Application	2,599 KB
CSV.kt	20/11/2017 10:57	KT File	2 KB
CSV.kt.bc	20/11/2017 11:47	BC File	10 KB

Run the program using the following command:

```
./CSV.exe books.csv 1
```

 The executable name might change slightly with different operating systems and different terminal or command prompts. It will also be different if you specify a different name for the output file when compiling.

It shows the following output:

```
MINGW64:/j/Work/Kotlin-Native/csv

Akshay@coderus MINGW64 /j/Work/Kotlin-Native/csv
$ ./CSV.exe books.csv 1
Coming soon -> 1
Published -> 4
```

Multiplatform Kotlin

A Kotlin multiplatform project allows you to compile the same code for multiple target platforms. Currently, supported target platforms are JVM and JS with Native, which is still under development and will be added later.

 Multiplatform Kotlin is still under review, similarly to Kotlin Native.

Project structure

A multiplatform project consists of three types of module—a common module, a platform module, and a regular module. Let's look at them in detail.

Common module

A `common` module contains platform-independent code, meaning it is not specific to any platform, as well as declarations without the implementation of platform-dependent APIs. Those declarations allow common code to depend on platform-specific implementations. This module is shared across other modules and is common between them, hence the name *common*.

A `common` module can depend only on other `common` modules and libraries, including the `kotlin-stdlib-common` Kotlin standard library .

A special *metadata* file is generated upon compiling the `common` module, which contains all the declarations in the module.

For example, let's say we need a `Date` object in Android, iOS, and web applications using the Kotlin Native project. All platforms have different implementations for getting the `Date` and `Time`. Hence, we can define our own `Date` class in our project, and its implementation will be in the platform-specific module.

The `common` module can only contain Kotlin code and cannot contain code in any other languages.

Platform module

A `platform` module contains the implementations of platform-dependent declarations in the `common` module for a specific platform, as well as other platform-dependent code. It is always an implementation of a single `common` module.

It can depend on any modules and libraries available on the given platform. This means that Java libraries can be used with Kotlin/JVM, and JS libraries with Kotlin/JS.

Upon compiling a `platform` module, it produces target-specific code (either JVM bytecode or JS source code) for the code in the `platform` module, as well as the `common` module that it implements.

There are several other languages targeting JVM; therefore, the platform modules targeting Kotlin/JVM can also contain code in Java and other JVM languages such as Scala.

Regular module

A `regular` module is a simple module that targets a specific platform. It can depend on platform modules or platform modules can depend upon it.

Hence, each multiplatform library needs to be distributed as a set of artifacts, as follows:

- A common `.jar` containing the metadata for common code
- Platform-specific `.jars` containing the compiled implementation code for each platform

Overview of the dependency structure

The following diagram shows the dependency structure of all the modules:

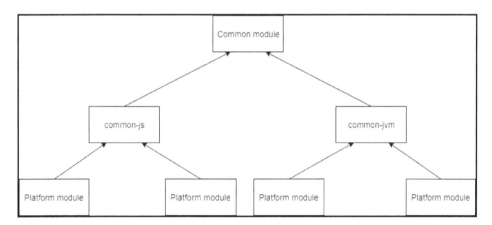

The following is a list of all the modules in the dependency structure:

- **Common module:** At the top of the chain is a single `common` module containing common code for all the platforms.
- **common-js:** This is an additional `common` module for JS-based platforms. It uses Kotlin/JS.
- **common-jvm:** This is an additional `common` module for JVM-based platforms. It uses Kotlin/JVM.
- **Platform module:** This contains platform-dependent code. For example, Android is a platform module whose parent is a `common-jvm` module.

Setting up a multiplatform project

Kotlin 1.2 adds new features to create a multiplatform project. They can only be built with Gradle; other build systems are not supported yet.

 Kotlin 1.2 is in the release candidate phase and should be stable pretty soon.

Creating a multiplatform project with an IDE

To create a new multiplatform project in the IDE, perform the following steps:

1. Open the **New Project** dialog.
2. Select the **Kotlin (Multiplatform)** option under **Kotlin**.
3. This will create a project with three modules—a common one and two platform ones for JVM and JS.

To add additional modules, perform the following steps:

1. Open the **New Module** dialog.
2. Select one of the **Kotlin (Multiplatform)** options under **Gradle**.

Creating a multiplatform project without an IDE

We can manually configure the project with Gradle by performing the following steps:

1. Create a Gradle project.
2. Add the Kotlin Gradle plugin to the build script `build.gradle` file: `classpath "org.jetbrains.kotlin:kotlin-gradle-plugin:$kotlin_version"`.
3. Apply the `kotlin-platform-common` plugin to the `common` module.
4. Add the `kotlin-stdlib-common` dependency to the `common` module.
5. Apply the `kotlin-platform-jvm` plugin for the JVM platform, and the `kotlin-platform-js` plugin for the JS platform.

The complete `build.gradle` file for a common module with Kotlin 1.2-Beta2 is as follows:

```
buildscript {
    ext.kotlin_version = '1.2-Beta2'

    repositories {
        maven { url 'http://dl.bintray.com/kotlin/kotlin-eap-1.2' }
        mavenCentral()
    }
    dependencies {
        classpath "org.jetbrains.kotlin:kotlin-gradle-
        plugin:$kotlin_version"
    }
}


apply plugin: 'kotlin-platform-common'

repositories {
    maven { url 'http://dl.bintray.com/kotlin/kotlin-eap-1.2' }
    mavenCentral()
}

dependencies {
    compile "org.jetbrains.kotlin:kotlin-stdlib-
      common:$kotlin_version"
    testCompile "org.jetbrains.kotlin:kotlin-test-
      common:$kotlin_version"
}
```

The complete `build.gradle` file for a JVM module with Kotlin 1.2-Beta2 is as follows:

```
buildscript {
    ext.kotlin_version = '1.2-Beta'

    repositories {
        maven { url 'http://dl.bintray.com/kotlin/kotlin-eap-1.2' }
        mavenCentral()
    }
    dependencies {
        classpath "org.jetbrains.kotlin:kotlin-gradle-
        plugin:$kotlin_version"
    }
}

apply plugin: 'kotlin-platform-jvm'

repositories {
    maven { url 'http://dl.bintray.com/kotlin/kotlin-eap-1.2' }
```

```
    mavenCentral()
}

dependencies {
    compile "org.jetbrains.kotlin:kotlin-stdlib:$kotlin_version"
    implement project(":")
    testCompile "junit:junit:4.12"
    testCompile "org.jetbrains.kotlin:kotlin-test-
      junit:$kotlin_version"
    testCompile "org.jetbrains.kotlin:kotlin-test:$kotlin_version"
}
```

Summary

Kotlin Native is definitely the future and we glimpsed what is possible in this chapter. But the language is still under review and there is a lot of stuff missing from it, such as documentation, better tooling support, and as well as a community, which I feel is the most important factor.

Multiplatform Kotlin enables the writing of Kotlin on Android, web, and iOS platforms respectively with the help of Native. It helps us reuse common code and have a single language across platforms.

We have successfully built our CSV reader application using the experimental Kotlin Native while leveraging amazing features such as interoperability with the C code, string interpolation, and extension functions. We also looked at how to compile the Kotlin code to a machine executable using the Kotlin Native compiler.

In the next chapter, we will look at how to build desktop applications using TornadoFX, which is based on a JavaFX Framework, with Kotlin features.

8

Dictionary Desktop Application - TornadoFX

As we have seen in `Chapter 7`, *CSV Reader in Kotlin Native*, the Kotlin Native technology will take some time to evolve. Further, programming with Kotlin Native is cumbersome and time-consuming because of the lack of any ecosystem that can be taken advantage of. All the other chapters in this book worked with either the Java ecosystem or the JavaScript ecosystem, both of which have been well developed over the years. We have seen how to build web applications (both client and server parts) as well as mobile applications. In this chapter, we shall cover how to create a desktop application using Kotlin. Again, we will be leveraging the Java ecosystem, which puts us back on the highway to go full speed towards development. On top of this, Kotlin's special constructs will further ease our work.

You will learn the following topics in this chapter:

- Setting up the development environment for TornadoFX
- Leveraging Kotlin-specific features for later development
- Using builders to create the user interface definition
- Consuming external API

Introducing TornadoFX

TornadoFX is a lightweight Kotlin framework around the JavaFX Framework. This means that it will run across all the hardware/operating systems supported by JavaFX, plus it will add Kotlin magic to simplify the coding for us developers.

Before we jump into TornadoFX, let's first understand where JavaFX fits into the scene.

Java-based desktop frameworks

The Java ecosystem is quite advanced in terms of the support it gives for building desktop applications. With the *write once, run anywhere* philosophy, the Java desktop applications are expected to work well on various heterogeneous platforms, such as Windows, macOS, and all Unix/Linux flavors—wherever a **Java virtual machine (JVM)** is available.

The Java ecosystem is rich with various flavors of desktop application framework. They are mentioned as follows:

- **Java AWT**: **AWT** stands for **advanced windowing toolkit**. AWT makes use of the native widgets of the underlying platform. This means that a desktop application running on a Windows platform will use Windows frames, dialogs, and controls, such as text boxes, and the same application, when deployed to Linux, will use the GNOME or KDE frames, dialogs, and controls. The JVM will make these components available to the application. A powerful layout mechanism lets the developer specify how the components are laid out with respect to one another, and, therefore, the applications will look good on different platforms, although the widths and heights of the controls will be different on them. As a limitation, AWT supports only those controls that are available on all the supported platforms; this means that users of a particular platform will miss using certain controls just because they may not be available on other platform.

- **Java Swing**: Swing is built upon the AWT machinery and uses the same layout mechanism, but its philosophy is completely opposite to AWT. Swing takes minimal features from the underlying platform—a little more than just the frames and dialogs and draws all the controls on them. Thus, Swing program support advanced controls (for example, JTable), irrespective of whether the underlying platform provides them or not, as these controls are simply created by the JVM. Because Swing has the liberty to draw the controls programmatically, it supports the pluggable look and feel, which can be applied to Swing application.

- **SWT**: **SWT** stands for **Standard Widget Toolkit**. While other desktop frameworks were developed at Sun, SWT was developed at IBM. SWT takes a middle path between AWT and Swing. It uses the Native platform widget whenever such a widget exists (like in AWT), but draws it in case it doesn't (like in Swing). This gives the best of both worlds. The SWT applications look completely native, but also support the richest set of controls.

- **JavaFX**: JavaFX is the modern desktop framework that was intended to be a replacement of Java Swing as the *standard* GUI library for Java. It is superior to Swing in terms of both the underlying technology (the ability to take advantage of hardware acceleration, handling touch, data binding) and capabilities (3D graphics, chart support, CSS3 styling, WebView support). A JavaFX UI can be built with object-oriented Java code or delegated to a specific XML file (this vocabulary is called FXML). The original plans for the JavaFX framework were very ambitious; it was intended to support not just desktop-based but also mobile-based and web-based applications. They were later dropped, although there are community attempts to use it beyond the desktop applications. For now, however, we shall look at it purely as a desktop application framework.

The main point to note here is that JavaFX stands tall upon a solid legacy. It is an improvement over what is already a highly sophisticated cross-platform GUI development environment. It is, therefore, one of the best frameworks to create cross-platform desktop applications.

TornadoFX special additions

What can Kotlin add to something that is perfect in the Java world? Plenty, as it turns out.

However, before we see what it could add, here is a quick point. Because of the complete interoperability with the Java ecosystem, Kotlin developers can use JavaFX out of the box without the need to use TornadoFX. However, there are merits in using Tornado FX.

Creating a type-safe UI versus FXML

As we mentioned previously, JavaFX offers two ways of building the UI—Java code and FXML.

The former is a type-safe way of building the UI. However, Java code is quite verbose and does not bring out the hierarchy of UI controls. In other words, it is not expressive enough. This is one of the major reasons that FXML is preferred in the JavaFX world.

TornadoFX turns this argument upside down. It utilizes Kotlin's expressive power to make the UI hierarchy explicit by looking at the code. It also brings the concept of builders, which leverage Kotlin's functional programming support and extension functions to produce UI code that is structured and easy to read. While the builders can be used with all controls, they especially shine when used with complex data controls, charts, shapes, and animations, which can be difficult (and verbose) to set up in a purely object-oriented way.

Because of this, *the use of a type-safe way of building the UI is preferred while working with TornadoFX*, unlike in JavaFX, where FXML is recommended. The advantages of creating the UI in a language (Java or Kotlin) while working with an **IDE (Integrated Development Environment)** are obvious:

- You get automated completion
- You get compilation-time type safety and type errors in the IDE before compiling

In Java FX, you use the `Stage` method and apply a `Scene` method to it. Tornado FX builds upon this to provide View, Controller, and Fragment components, which can be used in building the UI. Tornado FX provides dependency injection support so that these components can be easily referred to within one another. These facilities will make sense only with the type-safe way.

It may be noted that some developers will still want to work with FXML for other reasons:

- There is a WYSIWYG screen builder that simplifies the task of editing FXML. Some developers would like the ease of creating a UI using drag and drop tools.
- They may have existing FXML files and it would not be practical to redo them all with TornadoFX builders.

 Some articles on JavaFX state that it is easier to add multiple language support with FXML than with the Java coding. However, TornadoFX makes the task easy by supporting the `messages` construct, so this cannot be listed as a disadvantage of using type-safe coding.

TornadoFX can work with FXML and map the code to FXML-based GUI controls so that developers who want to work with FXML can still do so.

Type-safe styling

We saw earlier that JavaFX advocates the use of **CSS (Cascading Style Sheets)** to style the controls. While this is consistent with the web way of styling, it can be improved upon by using the type-safe CSS option provided by Tornado FX. In this way, the styles are expressed in pure Kotlin code instead of CSS.

You may notice that this is nothing but a **Domain Specific Language (DSL)**, which is possible in Kotlin because of its expressiveness.

A DSL is a language that is highly readable for the functional experts belonging to a domain. For example, a DSL may be used to define the UI (for the UI experts), and another DSL may be used to define test cases (for the testing experts). DSL uses the vocabulary of the underlying domain, and it is clean, in the sense that it is not littered by geeky-looking braces and semicolons; because of this, it is almost like plain English for the domain experts. They can easily understand and manipulate it. However, under the hood, it is the clever use of a highly expressive programming language in which domain-specific language constructs are defined adroitly so that the constructs are actually valid language constructs and they can be executed. One can see DSLs defined with Kotlin, Groovy, and Scala.

Here are some of the advantages you get by doing this:

- As with the UI definition, you get the advantages of compile-time type checking and autocompletion
- When both the styles and controls are coded in Kotlin, it is easy to filter controls and apply a given style to the filtered controls
- Another use case is to apply programmatic constructs such as mixins, for, say, using a base style in the definition of other styles

In the web world, one uses an SCSS or earlier version of stylesheet that transpiles to a CSS stylesheet to apply the programmatic constructs, at least in a limited fashion.

Other improvements

TornadoFX is built not for toy applications, but to develop robust, thread-safe, industry-strength applications. It gives a few facilities out of the box.

TornadoFX provides ViewModel, which is a mediator between the View and Model. While it provides a cleaner separation between the View and the Model of your application, it also gives you the functionality to roll back/commit or dirty state check out of the box. Think about the conventional implementation where this takes a lot of developer effort! All that gets saved with TornadoFX.

Another construct that TornadoFX provides for the programmer is to decouple the different components, such as Controller and View, is `EventBus`. With this, different components can pass messages to the `EventBus` library and read those that may be relevant to them.

Given that many desktop applications will work with some online resources, and given that the **REST (representational state transfer)** API is the de facto standard for data communication, TornadoFX ships with a REST API client and JSON support in built.

TornadoFX also adds a customizable wizard component. Some applications need to collect a large amount of data from users, typically in multiple chunks, and showing a wizard to the user is the preferred way of doing this. For such applications, the customizable wizard component is handy.

Let's build our dictionary application

We will build a dictionary application to understand how to build a desktop application using the TornadoFX framework, which is based on top of JavaFX framework. You will learn how to use TornadoFX and Kotlin to quickly build a robust and beautiful desktop application with features such as type-safe CSS.

The idea is to build a desktop-based dictionary application that shows the meaning(s) of the input word. It will fetch the meaning of the input word from the web using Words API.

What we will build

Here is a sneak peek of the application and how it will look and work until we reach the end of the chapter:

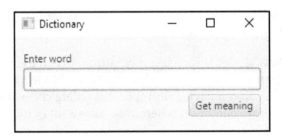

After the user enters the word and clicks on the **Get meaning** button, the meaning will be shown as follows:

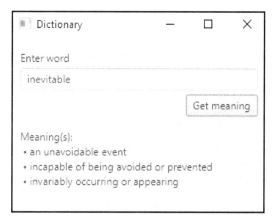

Words API

The dictionary application will fetch the meanings of a given word from the Words API site (https://www.wordsapi.com/). There are several APIs provided by the Words API website, but we will be using only the dictionary API to fetch the meaning.

You'll need to create an account on the Words API site (https://www.wordsapi.com/) to get the API key that we will use in the application. The process to create the account is pretty easy.

The Words API site provides lots of endpoints (APIs) for functions such as getting the synonyms, antonyms, and a lot more. We will be using its definition API.

Definition API

The definition API provides an endpoint to get the meaning of the word.

The following URL exposes the definitions API. We will call this URL with a GET request and pass the actual input word instead of {word}:

```
GET https://wordsapiv1.p.mashape.com/words/{word}/definitions
```

For example, to get the meaning of the word infinity the endpoint definition will be:

```
GET https://wordsapiv1.p.mashape.com/words/infinity/definitions
```

The following code snippet represents the request example:

```
curl --get --include
 'https://wordsapiv1.p.mashape.com/words/infinity/definitions' \
 -H 'X-Mashape-Key: YOUR_API_KEY' \
 -H 'Accept: application/json'
```

The following code line represents the response headers:

```
Content-Type: application/json
```

The following code snippet represents the response body:

```
{
  "word": "infinity",
  "definitions": [
    {
      "definition": "time without end",
      "partOfSpeech": "noun"
    }
  ]
}
```

When calling the definitions API, remember to pass the API key in the header as X-Mashape-Key to get a successful result.

Features of our application

The features in this application are as follows:

- User enters the input word
- User clicks on **Get meaning** to fetch the meaning of the input word

The following diagram represents the features in this application:

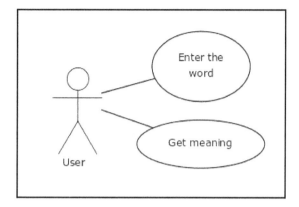

Setting up the IDE

Let's create the project in an IDE of our choice. I'm using IntelliJ Ultimate Edition to build the application. You can also use IntelliJ Community Edition, available from `https://www.jetbrains.com/idea/download/`.

Prerequisites

The prerequisites for this include the most recent version of IntelliJ IDEA Community Edition in Kotlin. The Gradle plugins should also be enabled (they should be enabled by default).

Installing the TornadoFX plugin

Follow the steps mentioned here to install the plugin:

1. Open the IDE settings.
2. Click on **Plugins**.
3. Open **Browse repositories**.
4. Search for `TornadoFX`.
5. Install the plugin and restart the IDE.

The following screenshot shows how to install the TornadoFX plugin:

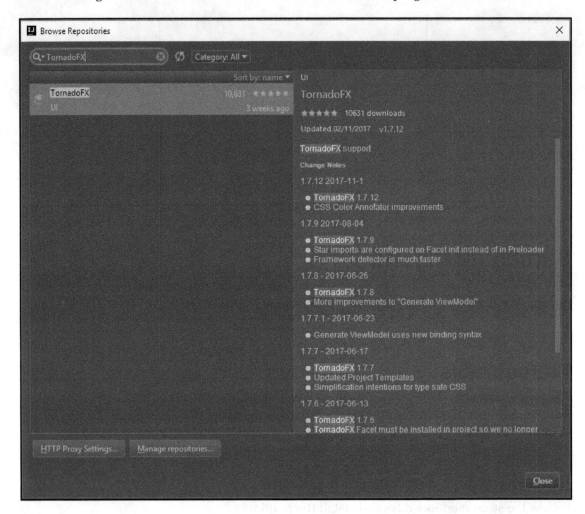

Creating the project

Create a new project in IntelliJ and select **TornadoFX** (this option is shown if the plugin is installed correctly), and then select `tornadofx-gradle-project` as shown in the following screenshot:

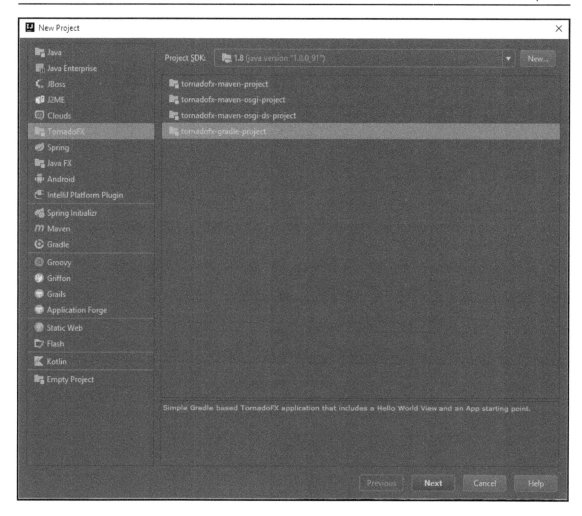

Selecting **TornadoFX** with **Gradle** automatically generates some starter code with a pre-filled Gradle script file— namely, `build.gradle`— and adds dependencies required by Kotlin and TornadoFX.

Project structure

The project structure contains the `main` module that holds our application code and its business logic.

The `main` module contains the `kotlin` directory (similar to Java) where all the Kotlin files are placed.

You don't have to put the Kotlin code into the `kotlin` directory, but it is a good convention to follow. If you place it under some other directory, then be sure to make the appropriate changes to `build.gradle`.

Here is the package structure with the base package as `com.akshay.dictionary` that we follow. Feel free to follow a similar structure in your projects. The following list shows the various elements of this structure:

- `app`: This contains the starting point of an app and its styling
- `controller`: This contains the logic to perform a REST call to the Words API dictionary
- `model`: This contains data classes required for JSON serialization and deserialization
- `view`: This contains the root layout of the app

The following screenshot represents the project explorer:

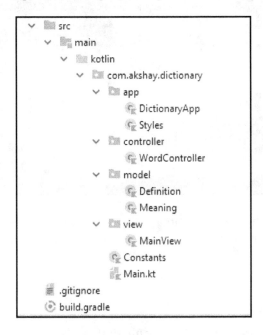

Let's code!

Our project is ready with the required project structure, Gradle dependency, and configuration. It's time to write the application code.

Application class

The `Application` class is the starting point, and there must be at least one class that extends the `App` class. It specifies the initial View that contains the display logic and layout of nodes that are managed as singleton:

```
/**
 * Starting point of the application
 */
class DictionaryApp : App(MainView::class, Styles::class)
```

We need to specify the primary View to the `App` class as the first constructor parameter. The second `Styles` parameter is optional and contains the `Stylesheet` method.

Type-safe CSS

TornadoFX provides type-safe CSS, which enables autocompletion, and checks at compilation time to conveniently create styles in its own class or provide inline styling. It's recommended to provide a `Stylesheet` method if you want to reuse and organize your styles. Take a look at the following code snippet:

```
class Styles : Stylesheet() {
  companion object {
    val appSizeRule by cssclass()
  }

  init {
    select(appSizeRule) {
      minHeight = 200.px
      minWidth = 300.px
    }
  }
}
```

We will create a rule to set the height and width of the application window and store `cssclass` in `companion object` so that it can be easily retrieved.

Dependency injection

Tornado FX supports dependency injection. However, you can also look up components using the `find` function:

```
val wordController = find(WordController::class)
```

When the `find` function is called, the component corresponding to the given class (`WordController`, in this case) is looked up in a global component registry. If it did not exist prior to the call, it will be created and inserted into the registry before the function returns.

The View and Controller are singletons; dependency injection is used to access the instance of a specific component.

The `inject` delegate is another mechanism to get the component in a lazy fashion. It is recommended to use the `inject` delegate as it's a lazy mechanism that means the actual instance will only be created the first time the variable is called. Also, it allows your components to have circular dependencies. Take a look at the following example:

```
val wordController: WordController by inject()
```

Property delegate

JavaFX has a special type called `Property`. It maintains a value internally and notifies listeners of its changes. It is unique to JavaFX because it supports binding operations and will notify the UI when it changes.

 The JavaFX `Property` delegate is different from Kotlin's standard property delegation. Don't confuse it with the standard property delegation of Kotlin.

Let's look at the following example, where we will define a JavaFX property of type `String` and delegate the getters and setters directly from the property:

```
class Meaning {
  val wordProperty = SimpleStringProperty()
  var word by wordProperty
}
```

Consuming the REST API

The JSON format has become the de facto standard when working with REST APIs, and TornadoFX provides support for JSON and REST in two forms:

- Enhancements to the `javax.json` objects and functions
- A specialized REST client to perform automatic conversion between JSON and your domain models

To enable this conversion between JSON and domain models, the domain model classes need to implement the `JsonModel` interface.

Defining the Model

We will define the `Model` as per the response JSON received from the Words API website. Let's take a look at the following code:

```
class Meaning {

    val wordProperty = SimpleStringProperty()
    var word by wordProperty

    val definitions = FXCollections.observableArrayList<Definition>()
}
```

Implementing the JSONModel interface

We will implement the `JsonModel` interface to facilitate the conversion between JSON and the domain classes, for which we will need to override two functions—`updateModel` and `toJSON`.

The `updateModel` function is called to convert the JSON object to the domain model. It receives a JSON object as a parameter from which we update the properties of our domain model object. Let's take a look at the following example:

```
override fun updateModel(json: JsonObject) {
  with(json) {
    word = string("word")
    definitions.setAll(getJsonArray("definitions").toModel())
  }
}
```

The `toJSON` function is called to convert the domain model object to a JSON payload. It receives `JsonBuilder` as a parameter where we set the values of the model object and create a JSON file using the builder. Take a look at the following example:

```
override fun toJSON(json: JsonBuilder) {
  with(json) {
    add("word", word)
    add("definitions", definitions.toJSON())
  }
}
```

After implementing `JsonModel`, our `Meaning` class looks like this:

```
class Meaning : JsonModel {

  val wordProperty = SimpleStringProperty()
  var word by wordProperty

  val definitions = FXCollections.observableArrayList<Definition>()

  override fun updateModel(json: JsonObject) {
    with(json) {
      word = string("word")
      definitions.setAll(getJsonArray("definitions").toModel())
    }
  }

  override fun toJSON(json: JsonBuilder) {
    with(json) {
      add("word", word)
      add("definitions", definitions.toJSON())
    }
  }
}
```

Similarly, we will define the `Definition` class as per the JSON structure we receive from the Words API as follows:

```
class Definition : JsonModel {

  val definitionProperty = SimpleStringProperty()
  var definition by definitionProperty

  val partOfSpeechProperty = SimpleStringProperty()
  var partOfSpeech by partOfSpeechProperty

  override fun updateModel(json: JsonObject) {
    with(json) {
```

```
      definition = string("definition")
      partOfSpeech = string("partOfSpeech")
    }
  }

  override fun toJSON(json: JsonBuilder) {
    with(json) {
      add("definition", definition)
      add("partOfSpeech", partOfSpeech)
    }
  }

  override fun toString(): String {
    return definition
  }

}
```

REST client

TornadoFX comes with a REST client that makes it easy to perform JSON-based REST calls.

The underlying HTTP engine interface has two implementations:

- By default, it uses `HttpURLConnection`
- Apache `HttpClient`

To change the HTTP engine to the Apache `HttpClient` implementation, we will simply need to call `Rest.useApacheHttpClient()` in the `init` block of the `App` class.

 Make sure that you add extra dependency `org.apache.httpcomponents:httpclient` in the project description or the Gradle file to use the Apache HTTP client.

Configuring the client

As we will always access the same API. We can set a base URL in the client. Also, for every request that is made, the Words API requires an API key in the header, for which we set the request interceptor to make sure every request sent using the client will contain the API key in the header.

We will perform this configuration in the `init` block. It can be added to the `App` class or the primary View as follows:

```
// Get the REST client
private val api: Rest by inject()

init {
  // Configuring the client
  api.baseURI = "https://wordsapiv1.p.mashape.com/words/"
  api.engine.requestInterceptor = {
    (it as HttpURLRequest).addHeader("X-Mashape-Key",
    Constants.WORDS_API_KEY)
  }
}
```

We have stored the Words API key in a separate Kotlin file named `Constants`. Make sure that you store your API key securely in your project.

Controllers

Controllers are the middleman between View and Model. They contain the convenience functions, such as performing basic HTTP operations such as GET, PUT, POST, and DELETE. They add an abstraction layer and help separate the networking logic from our business logic or the UI logic.

Here, we have a `WordController` class that contains a function named `getMeaning`, which sends a GET request to the Words API in order to get the meaning of the specified word, and on a success, it receives a response that the REST client internally converts to a domain model object; otherwise, else it returns `null`:

```
/**
 * Abstraction layer to perform HTTP operations
 */
class WordController : Controller() {

  private val api: Rest by inject()

  /**
   * Sends a GET request to fetch the meaning
   * from the API endpoint
   * @param word to get the meaning for
   * @return meaning object if success else null
   */
```

```
fun getMeaning(word: String): Meaning? {
  val response = api.get("$word/definitions")
  try {
    return when {
      response.ok() -> response.one().toModel()
      else -> null
    }
  } finally {
    response.consume()
  }
}
}
```

The `api.get` function performs an HTTP GET request and returns a `Response` object. Then we call `one()` or `list()`, depending on whether the JSON response is a single object or a list, which will convert the response to `JsonObject` or `JsonArray`.

Next, we will call the extension function, `JsonObject.toModel()`, that creates one object of the `Meaning` class, as per the `JsonObject` method. Internally, it calls `JsonModel.updateModel()`, which means `Meaning.updateModel()` is called.

Lastly, we will call `response.consume()` to clean up the resources when the request fails.

Views

The primary View is the default View that is set when the application is opened. It is set in the `App` class, which does the job of loading this View when the app opens.

Every View needs to override the `root` property, which contains the layout for the View. The `root` property contains a hierarchy of JavaFX nodes (which are kind of View methods).

The following is an example of a View with an empty layout:

```
class MainView : View("Dictionary") {
  override val root = vbox {
    // Contains the View hierarchy
  }
}
```

It will show an empty window with the title of **Dictionary**.

Layouts

TornadoFX supports a lot of layouts that can help you to build a complex UI. They provide controls such as grouping, positioning, and sizing with set policies, with support for type-safe builders to create layouts in a highly structured and declarative way, and Kotlin really shines in this department.

VBox layout

A VBox stacks the controls or the nodes vertically, in the order that they are declared inside its block. Take a look at the following example:

```
vbox {
    button("Button A")
    button("Button B")
}
```

This image illustrates the vbox shown in the preceding code:

HBox layout

A HBox is very similar to a VBox. It stacks all controls or nodes horizontally, left to right, in the order declared in its block. Take a look at the following example:

```
hbox {
    button("Button A")
    button("Button B")
}
```

This image illustrates the hbox shown in the preceding code:

Other layouts

Similarly, there is the `FlowPane` layout, which lays out controls from left to right and wraps them to the next line on the boundary, and the `BorderPane` layout, which is a highly useful layout that divides the controls into five regions: top, left, bottom, right, and center.

Forms

TornadoFX comes with `Form` control to deal with handling a large number of user inputs; having several input fields to take information from the user such as login or register is common.

You can create a `form` with any number of fields using the form builder. Creating a `form` is similar to creating the View, except the parent is the form layout.

In the following code, we show a form that is used to get the input word from the user and a button to get the meaning from the web:

```
form {
    fieldset(labelPosition = Orientation.VERTICAL) {
        field("Enter word", Orientation.VERTICAL) {
            inputWord = textfield()
        }
        buttonbar {
            button("Get meaning") {
                action {
                    // Click event
                }
            }
        }
    }
}
```

Each `field` represents a container with the label and another container for the input fields you add inside it. You can specify the `orientation` function as a parameter to a field to make it lay out multiple inputs after each other; this allows the input form to grow vertically.

You can use the `buttonbar` builder to create a special field with no label while retaining the label indent so that the buttons line up under the inputs.

Background operations

We don't want to block our UI when our app is performing a long-running operation, such as performing a network call or any database operations, because it makes the app unresponsive, which is inefficient and makes the end users unhappy.

Fortunately, TornadoFX provides the runAsync function. Any code placed inside a runAsync block will run in the background. If, say, the result from the background is required to update the UI that needs to be performed on JavaFX's application thread, then the ui block comes to the rescue.

The result of the runAsync function is available in the ui block, which can be used to update the UI.

In the following code snippet, we send an HTTP request in the background using the runAsync function and update the UI in the ui block:

```
runAsync {
  // Send request to API
  controller.getMeaning(inputWord.text)
} ui { meaning ->
// Update the UI
  }
```

Printing the result

When the user clicks on **Get meaning**, we will need to get the input word from the input field so that we can fetch its meaning. For this reason, let's keep the instance of the input field in a global state. We also need a label to print the result when the meaning is fetched from the API.

We will make these variables global as the actual values will be assigned later as a format known as a delegation. We can use the lateinit modifier, but TornadoFX comes with a singleAssign delegate that mimics the behavior of lateinit, but it doesn't result in a crash, and tells the compiler that the value will only be assigned once. It is also thread safe and helps mitigate issues with mutability represented by the following lines of code:

```
// UI elements
private var inputWord: TextField by singleAssign()
private var result: Label by singleAssign()
```

Later, we will use these global field variables that are assigned only once to manipulate the UI, as shown here, where we are printing the input word and then printing the meaning:

```
// Print the input word
println(inputWord.text)

// Getting the meaning ....

// Process and print the result on the UI
val meanings = meaning.definitions.joinToString("\n • ", "\n • ") {
it.definition
}
result.text = "Meaning(s): $meanings"
```

Complete View

Here is our primary `View/MainView/` that contains the complete code of the `View` explained in bits and pieces:

```
/**
 * Base view shown when the application is started
 */
class MainView : View("Dictionary") {

  // Get the REST client
  private val api: Rest by inject()
  private val controller: WordController by inject()

  // UI elements
  private var inputWord: TextField by singleAssign()
  private var result: Label by singleAssign()

  init {
    // Configuring the client
    api.baseURI = "https://wordsapiv1.p.mashape.com/words/"
    api.engine.requestInterceptor = {
      (it as HttpURLRequest).addHeader("X-Mashape-Key",
      Constants.WORDS_API_KEY)
    }
  }

  /**
   * Root View
   */
  override val root = vbox {
    addClass(cssRule)
```

```
form {
    fieldset(labelPosition = Orientation.VERTICAL) {
        field("Enter word", Orientation.VERTICAL) {
            inputWord = textfield()
        }
        buttonbar {
            button("Get meaning") {
                action {
                    runAsync {
                        // Send request to API
                        controller.getMeaning(inputWord.text)
                    } ui { meaning ->
                        if (meaning != null) {
                            // Show the result on the UI
                            val meanings = meaning.definitions.joinToString(
                            "\n • ",
                            "\n • ") { it.definition }
                            result.text = "Meaning(s): $meanings"
                        } else {
                            result.text = "Unable to find the meaning"
                        }
                    }
                }
            }
        }
    }
    // Result
    result = label { }
}
}
}
```

Launching the application

Launching the application is pretty easy and there are several ways to do it. The easiest way to run the application is as follows:

1. Open your `App` class (in our case, the `DictionaryApp` class).
2. Click on the Tornado icon near the line number.
3. Click on **Run**.

The following screenshot shows how to run the application:

```
     Run 'DictionaryApp'          Ctrl+Shift+F10
     Debug 'DictionaryApp'                          the application
     Run 'DictionaryApp' with Coverage

     class DictionaryApp : App(MainView::class, Styles::class)
```

The tornado icon is shown only if you have installed the TornadoFX plugin. It is highly recommended that you do install.

Summary

TornadoFX is a lightweight framework that you can use to quickly build beautiful desktop applications while leveraging the amazing features of Kotlin and JavaFX framework, but, as far as the capabilities are concerned, it's a real tornado.

As you have seen in this chapter, we proved that we can create beautiful and maintainable applications. The beauty of TornadoFX is that it unlocks a whole new level of concise and beautiful code without hiding any features of JavaFX. The principal design goal is to facilitate beautiful, concise, and readable Kotlin code—a DSL-like approach—and to cut boilerplate code to the absolute minimum.

TornadoFX adds some very useful extensions to the JavaFX UI family including wizard, form, datagrid, drawers, and so on. It is compatible with other libraries you may add to your application, such as ReactFX, RxJavaFX, and Kovenant.

Right from the beginning, TornadoFX supports popular design patterns such as MVC, MVP, and MVVM. The beauty is that using them is not imposed on the programmers.

With FXML and FXID delegates and type-safe builders, you can clearly see how much you can gain. You get built-in dependency injection. There is first-class support for JSON and convenient conversions. All these contribute to saving time and improving developer productivity.

Index

www.ingramcontent.com/pod-product-compliance
Lightning Source LLC
Chambersburg PA
CBHW080635060326
40690CB00021B/4936